The Manager's Diary

Thinking Outside The Cubicle

Cameron Morrissey

For Jasmine and Alex

Together you are my North Star, guiding me through the journey

TABLE OF CONTENTS

Hiding in Plain Sight:
Obvious Things We're Too Busy To Notice

The Staff:
Managing For Success

Great Talent:
Hard To Find & Tough To Develop

Yourself:
If You Can't Mange Yourself, You're In Trouble

Projects:
When All Eyes Are Watching

Team:
You're A Player Not Just A Coach

The Customer:
The Reason You Have A Job

Appendix I
A Management Compare & Contrast

Appendix II
Five Great Debates

Appendix III
Top 100 Leadership Quotes

Preface

After making a few too many mistakes for the second (and often third or fourth) time, and after passing off bits of wisdom more regularly to my staff, I decided to start writing down what I was learning on the job day in and day out. Eventually, as the list got longer and longer I started blogging the choicest thoughts and lessons. This led to Twitter and Facebook Pages, then Tumblr and LinkedIn.

But one of the goals I always set out for myself was to write a book. This book represents the sum parts of my learning over the course of a year. Each article has been updated, revised, and added to with the benefit of even more wisdom.

Introduction

Reading is great, gaining wisdom is fantastic, but only by putting our lessons into action do we truly drive performance improvements. With that in mind, you will find a "LESSON ASSIGNMENT" at the end of each chapter. It is here where you have the opportunity to grow in your management style and your career.

We all have different ways of tackling a book like this: Some methodically read one chapter a day, some "binge read" and tackle it all at once, and other "hunt and peck" their way through whatever parts of the book interest them and leave the rest. None is particularly better than another, it's simply personal preference.

Let me challenge you, however, to set a goal of putting these lesson assignments into action. Regardless of your reading style you can play along. Every week, look to put the following amount of lesson assignments into practice at your place of work:

- **Director Level:** One Lesson Assignment p/week
- **Vice President Level:** Two Lesson Assignments p/week
- **CEO Level:** Three Lesson Assignments p/week

So whether you read the whole book in one night or only read the titles that interest you, set a goal of putting 1-3 of the lesson assignments into practical action in your place of work. Do this consistently every week and I'm confident you will see an impact on both yourself and your staff.

Hiding in Plain Sight:
Obvious Things We're Too Busy To Notice

The Manager's Diary

Don't Clarify The Problem, Find The Solution

Diary Entry #18 – May 28th

"Good management is the art of making problems so interesting and their solutions so constructive that everyone wants to get to work and deal with them." ~Paul Hawken

"The problem at this point is that there is a problem." ~Captain Obvious

. . . . .

Stop stating the obvious and get focused on solutions. I can't tell you how much time and energy is spent either simply reiterating the problem or re-clarifying minute details of the issue. Why does this occur so often? Well it is easier to talk than to fix the problem for one, but there are three big reasons:

- *Political* - The person wants to appear to be part of the discussion, especially if everyone's boss is on the distribution of the e-mail.
- *No Answer* - The individual doesn't have anything constructive to contribute. The lowest common denominator of solution finding is pointing out what doesn't work.

- *Stalling* - Excuses by the project lead or a stakeholder as to why they haven't met the deadline.

Now of course, this is not meant to stop the understanding of a problem. To effectively solve the issue, you need to understand it. What I am talking about here is the prevalence of comments that do not add to the understanding. Phrases that generally, but don't always, indicate that the words that follow may be a waste of breath or typeface:

- "The problem is…"
- "What we need is…"
- "Don't forget that…"

This wastes time in seeking resolution, or worse yet, misdirects the discussion onto a peripheral issue. Either way, it is grossly unproductive.

This also occurs with those who shoot down solutions or poke holes in others. To these people, I recommend you answer with a solid "What would you recommend?" Used consistently, this often either shuts the person up who continues to exercise this type of behavior, or in the best case scenario, actually focuses them on coming up with their own ideas.

If you can cut out the amount of wasted time reclarifying the issue everyone knows about and instead focus on ideas for solving it, you have dramatically sped up the solution timeline.

If there is a problem with someone's solution, a solution to that NEW problem should be initiated. With enough practice within an organization, momentum builds toward problem solving so that things get done in DRASTICALLY less time.

LESSON ASSIGNMENT: The next time that you propose an idea, add the following line at the end of your e-mail to focus the discussion:

"Please don't comment on why the idea may not work, only comment with how to make this idea work, or propose your own idea."

Don't Just Focus on the Poor Performers

Diary Entry #9 – May 7th

"A good objective of leadership is to help those who are doing poorly to do well and those who are doing well to do even better." ~Jim Rohn

"Most organizations staff their problems & starve their opportunities." ~Peter Drucker

· · · · ·

In business, our natural inclination is to focus on the problem and find a solution to it. In effect, we move from problem to problem, solving as we go. This works just fine, but you're missing out on a HUGE amount of opportunities through this myopic thinking. Nowhere is this more prevalent than in the management of staff. Of course, your poor performers need to be coached to perform better, but why are you forgetting about the other 80 percent of your staff that is doing well or even excelling???

- Your best performers are often the ones that respond best to coaching, which means you'll often see a more immediate improvement than with the poorer performers.

- Your best performers usually have more "tricks of the trade" that can be shared amongst the staff, and more feedback to give you on what you need to do to improve the operation.
- Your best performers also set the bar for the rest of the staff, so if you want to raise the bar, start with them.

With that being said, you must deal with your best performers in a different way than your poor performers. While your poor performers may need more training, more structure, and more coaching, your best performers need more:

- o Recognition
- o Praise
- o Team-Building

Pulling some of your focus away from your poor performers to address some of the three items listed above with your best performers is time VERY well spent. One of the best ways to accomplish all three at the same time is to set up bi-weekly meeting for your best performers to brainstorm challenges and opportunities in the department. You can preside over the meeting, but it is really for your people to run the agenda.

Beyond these three items though, your best performing employees want **Meaningful and Challenging Work**. If they are bored and feel that their work has no impact on the operation/department then they will lose focus. It is important that you give them important work and reinforce that sense of importance so as to retain them. One of the reasons I have moved on in my work is that I felt I could make a more meaningful contribution elsewhere. Some of your best employees may be considering the same. Bring them into the heart of what you do and watch them flourish.

Now this isn't to say you should neglect the poor performers, or for goodness sake, the middle of the road performers. It is just to illustrate that there is a lot of improvement waiting to be unleashed by your ENTIRE staff, and the biggest improvements don't always lie in your poorest performers. So keep measuring your best performers, put your best performers next to one another to "shadow", make sure your best performers go through training as well. You'll be surprised by the results.

LESSON ASSIGNMENT: Pull your three best employees into a room together and ask them how they are so successful? What tools do they use? What tips would they give a new coworker? Then disseminate the information to your entire staff.

How to Salvage a Pointless Meeting

Diary Entry #20 – June 3rd

"Meetings are indispensable when you don't want to do anything." ~John
Kenneth Galbraith

"People who enjoy meetings should not be in charge of anything." ~Thomas
Sowell

•   •   •   •   •

Let's face it, meetings suck. But the terrible thing about it….the
higher you move up in the corporate food chain, the more you'll
be invited to. And even worse….the higher you move up in the
corporate food chain the less time you have to waste on
pointless meetings.

Politically, you have little choice but to attend. Meetings give you
face time, and often help to establish the interpersonal
relationships necessary to help you get your job done, but they're
still more often than not, a colossal waste of time. So what to
do?

Now some people do the common thing, and just tune out in
meetings. You can recognize them by their distinctive natural cry

for help when they are asked a question and respond, "I'm sorry, what was the question again?" But this is an egregious mistake, both to your career and the enterprise at large.

What I do when I'm called to a meeting that turns out to be a waste of time? I look to do three things when it becomes obvious that it is going to be a waste:

1. *Lend my expertise to try move the project/initiative the meeting is about along* - This one is your duty to your peers and the organization. You can't just tune out (unfortunately), you have an obligation to see to it that the meeting has some value.
2. *Keep a pad of paper around to write down any ideas come into my head about my own projects/department/initiatives* - This is just a trick I learned from too many meetings where there is dead space and I can "get away in my own head" to think about what I would be working on if I weren't in this darn conference room. By writing it down quickly, I can reengage the meeting without losing the points being made.
3. *Get at least one thing out of the meeting* - This is the purpose of this post. If you pay attention and look for lessons to learn (from superiors, peers, and subordinates, you can almost always pick out a few things that can help you in managing your department, help the organization, or help you in your career

Common things I find when looking to get at least one thing out of a meeting:

- Lessons other managers have learned
- Struggles within the organization where my department can make a difference
- Management philosophy

- What stakeholders in future endeavors really care about (getting a feel for their thinking can be essential to finding allies to get your ideas across)

I've been able to pull one good "point three" thing out of almost every meeting I've attended in the last year and a half with my current company, and I'm sure this can change what is usually a waste of your day, into something at least modestly beneficial.

LESSON ASSIGNMENT: For each meeting you have this week, look to accomplish two things:

- Make a meaningful contribution to the meeting, either in insight and/or refocusing it on its purpose.
- Learn at least one thing to improve your career or understanding of the business.

An Easy Way to Spot Dumb Processes and Tools

Diary Entry #28 – July 2nd

"I put my heart and my soul into my work, and have lost my mind in the process. " ~Vincent Van Gogh

"Simplicity is the ultimate sophistication" ~Leonardo da Vinci

.   .   .   .   .

When you are looking to help your people so they can do their job better, you have to look at their tools and the processes surrounding them. I recommend you ask yourself one simple question: Is it better than what they could come up with themselves or buy for their own use at home? Trust me, your employees are asking the same question.

Your employees want to do a good job, and they want to do it as quickly and easily as possible (If not, well, you've got bigger problems than I can cover here). When they see obvious areas of needed improvement they will usually speak up because it seems so ridiculous to them. Here's a couple of good examples:

- Is your company's Intranet faster than broadband at home?

- Do they have access to equipment quickly and cost effectively?
    - How long does it take to get a replacement computer in your company? They can buy one at Best Buy on their lunch break.
- Do you have access to a wide variety of materials quickly and cost efficiently?
    - I've had it take 3 weeks to get a can of paint I could have gone to Home Depot and bought for the same price in 30 minutes.
- What about apps? Have you tapped into that market yet?

If the answer is "no" to most of these questions, then your company is at a strategic disadvantage to its competitors.

But how do you do it? It's not like companies are set up for this level of flexibility usually, otherwise there wouldn't be an issue in the first place. To actually put some of these good things in place once you've identified them requires four things as I see it:

1) A "thinking outside the box" attitude
    a. You'll most likely be doing something different than what has usually been done in the company. So be ready to break some molds.
2) An understanding of the process as it stands now
    a. You can't understand the impact of your change (positive and negative) if you don't understand how the process works now.
3) An ability to show an accurate ROI
    a. If you're looking to add new tools or do things a different way than the "Standard Operating Procedure" you need to show what the return is on the change. If there isn't a savings in money (or time) you aren't going to get far.
4) And usually a reasonable boss

a. Usually these changes/tools are not rocket science, but they are different, and different is dangerous to many bosses.

So ask whether the tools your people are using at work are better than what they have at home, or whether the processes are better than what they could do themselves. Use this as a baseline and you'll identify some immediate opportunities for improvement.

LESSON ASSIGNMENT: Ask your employees what the Top 5 silliest technological or process related things are that should be easily fixed (their idea of easy is usually different than our reality). Put together the list ranked by most number of "votes". Select three that are doable, and see what magic you can work.

Learn From Your Bitchiest Employees

Diary Entry #4 - April 30th

"The wildest colts make the best horses." ~*Plutarch*

"Your most unhappy customers are your greatest source of learning." ~*Bill Gates*

. . . . .

So we all know who they are. If there were a handful of employees that we would intentionally avoid, they are the ones….the complainers. You work your butt off and they still complain, you fix things and they still complain, you try something new and they complain, you keep things the same and they complain. It's demoralizing and one of the tougher things to deal with as a manager. But if you think of your complaining employees as you think of your complaining customers, you realize that they are a resource to show you where you need to improve most.

People will tell you what they need, whether they be customers or employees. They want to be heard and have the ability to have their say in what goes on around them. Yes, some complain just for the sake of complaining, but employees want the tools and resources to do their job better (satisfying the customer) and easier (satisfying themselves). Similar to customers, your most vocal complainers are most likely saying what your other employees won't, and they are the easiest resource for determining where there are deficiencies in their tools and the operation as a whole. So when you start to listen, what you'll hear that is vital to your improvement:

- The barriers they are encountering regularly.
- The barriers that "should" be easily fixable (they may not understand the complications to the solution).
- The barriers that cause them the most pain.
- What the customers are saying about your product and service.

After finding out what their problems are with how things are done, it's simply a matter of selecting what can be fixed, and prioritize those fixes. So while you may not be able to win them over, they can still be one of your most valuable tools in the effort to improve your department's performance. Don't be afraid, or discouraged, in using them.

The other phenomenon that can occur is that you will encourage other employees to begin giving their feedback as well. Now hopefully this just increases the amount of feedback you receive from your staff and doesn't just turn into a constant flow of griping. In the end, what will determine the direction it goes is you and how you act on the feedback you receive.

LESSON ASSIGNMENT: Start a Top 10 list of the complaints your bitchiest employees make. Once you have 10 items, choose the three easiest ones to fix. Once those are fixed add three more items to the list, then fix two. Replace those two with two more, then fix one. Once done, wad up the list and throw it away.

Then pull together a meeting of your top complainers and review the six items you addressed and ask for a new Top 10 list and repeat the process. The reason to start over is that your list may get clogged with "unfixable" things like wages and vacation time, or what you thought was fixed turns out to not be fixed. But most importantly, as your employees see some items fixed, what they see as problems may change. They therefore begin to prioritize their own complaints as they see progress.

Be Able to Sprint, But Realize Nobody Can Sprint Forever

Diary Entry #40 – August 16th

"One of the tests of leadership is the ability to recognize a problem before it becomes an emergency." ~Arnold Glasow

"A clever person solves a problem. A wise person avoids it" ~Albert Einstein

.   .   .   .   .

We see it all the time, something occurs in the business environment and we have to "knuckle down", "call in the troops", and/or "burn the midnight oil". This is a natural occurrence and should be expected from time to time. But the concerns come in when these things happen more regularly.

When "knuckling down" becomes the standard practice, when "burning the midnight oil" becomes a regular occurrence, then to use another set of buzzwords, you risk the "wheels coming off of the bus". The fact is that people will either stop treating the emergencies with the urgency they should (they become accustomed to the state of affairs), or they burn out and your turnover starts climbing. Either one of these scenarios eventually leads to the "wheels falling off" of your bus.

- Are your part-timers working full-time hours?
- Is your equipment so busy that you do not have enough downtime for routine maintenance?
- Are your supervisors not taking vacation or are they coming in on their days off?
- Are your service levels experiencing routine declines during certain days of the week, or times of day?
- Is your turnover increasing?

Again, you need to be able to put the "petal to the metal" when business demands it, but you simply cannot, as a responsible manager, set up the structure of your department to rely on the extra effort/strain on a regular basis. To do so is irresponsible. Sometimes there is a natural high that comes from overcoming an emergency, but don't fall into the trap of becoming addicted to it. Some things to look at:

- *Look for the root cause of the extra work.* Is it poor planning or scheduling? Do your people have the right training and tools?
- *Are expectations reasonable?* Does the timeline reflect reality, is the amount of work expected from each individual reasonable or "ideal".

Work overload cannot become a status quo within your department if you want your staff to excel. Fight it off in every way you can.

LESSON ASSIGNMENT: If you find yourself in a situation where the staff is "fried", find a way to give at least one week where the staff is not under pressure. Letting the pressure off for even a short bit of time will help. Alternatively, take the staff offsite for a long lunch, something social like a pizza parlor or bowling alley, where you can eat and have fun. These little things go a long way for endurance.

When Something Goes Right, Repeat It

Diary Entry #48 – September 14th

"3 Rules of Work: Out of clutter find simplicity; From discord find harmony; In the middle of difficulty lies opportunity." ~Albert Einstein

"Close scrutiny will show that most "crisis situations" are opportunities to either advance, or stay where you are." ~Maxwell Maltz

.   .   .   .   .

Let's be honest, we're all working, planning, and creating initiatives to improve the business, but oftentimes some of the best results occur with little planning or occur almost by accident. The key is to follow up the surprising opportunities with a repeat performance.

This came to mind for me recently when we were anticipating a VERY busy week, with almost double the usual volume. What happened was that we sent people from Marketing, Sales, and other areas that don't usually interact with the customers directly to the front line of the operation (we asked for volunteers so we got the right people). It was a huge success, with customer satisfaction and employee satisfaction/stress heading in the right direction. But we were about to let it go as a "once a year" sort of scenario until one manager asked "why don't we do that every time we expect more business"? Simple logic, but everyone was missing it, they weren't looking for the opportunity.

If you do something, even in a crisis, and it works, ask yourself if you can do it again

Successes are tough to find sometimes, so if one falls into your lap, see if you can leverage it again. The keys are:

- *Notice the success* – In the example above, we were all focused on "getting back to business" and normal operations. Only one of us identified the opportunity. The first key is to notice what is going on around you and what is working. I know we are all supposed to be looking, but sometimes it's not exactly where you are focused, so be sure you are surveying the entire scene.
- *Does it need to be tweaked* – Can the success be improved upon, or does it need an adjustment to mold itself into a repeatable process.
- *Roll it out and observe* – Sometimes the success was the result of something else, so be sure to observe it better the second time and see if it is still working and what can be learned and improved.

Whether it is the music playing in the background, the hours of operation, the color of your sales clerk's uniforms, all that matters is that it works. So look for those opportunities, then immediately look to repeat them.

LESSON ASSIGNEMNT: Think back on the last several crisis situations your department faced (usually sale days, product rollout, a bunch of sick calls, etc). Were you able to come up with a plan that was successful in addressing the issue? If so, then ask yourself whether it can be rolled out at other times to make improvements.

Why Your Idiot Boss Is Successful

Diary Entry #5 – May 1st

"Leadership is difficult but it is not complex." ~Michael McKinney

"The business schools reward difficult complex behavior more than simple behavior, but simple behavior is more effective." ~Warren Buffett

. . . . .

We've all been there. Our boss, or at least our "friend's" boss (if we're being evasive) is a complete idiot. They can't follow directions to the meeting, can't figure out how to reschedule a meeting in Outlook, can't spell, and generally don't have an understanding of how the world works. But they are actually fairly successful within the organization and continue to see promotions. How can this be? They have realized what so few see:

BUSINESS IS SIMPLE

I didn't say it was easy, I said it was simple. People without the capacity for complicated thought (like your less than intelligent boss) are forced to simplify things. As many of us know, simplifying things is one of the hallmarks of great management.

The stupid boss does not have the capacity to actually overcomplicate things and so they don't.

- Revenue needs to increase – sell more products and sell higher value products.
- Costs need to be cut – where can we cut them?
- The Vice President wants something done now – they drop everything and do whatever it is RIGHT NOW.

They don't think about complicated analyses determining underlying metrics of productivity, they simply work in a knee-jerk way. It is generally quick and directed, hallmarks of any good decision making. Now this doesn't work in every organization (hopefully doctors don't fit into this model), but it can work in most up to certain points. So the next time you're in a meeting with your peers from other divisions and one of them is a complete moron, yet inexplicably still has the trust of the President, ask yourself whether you can actually learn something about simplicity from them.

Now you're saying "But Cameron wait, that isn't everything it takes to be a leader", and you're right, it isn't. These bosses do not plan well, and based on that, tend to sacrifice the long term for the short term gain. But rightly or wrongly, that is often what gets noticed by the superiors who feel it is their responsibility to manage the "long term". So remember the K.I.S.S. Principle: Keep It Simple Stupid. It has led to the success of many of our superiors.

LESSON ASIGNMENT: The next time your boss says to do something, do it immediately then report back to him/her. Don't prioritize it with what you are currently working on, don't question the legitimacy of the task, just do it. Try it out and see both how it feels, and the reaction from your boss.

The Staff:
Managing For Success

Feedback Should Go Both Ways

Diary Entry #8 – May 6th

"Truly great leaders spend as much time collecting and acting upon feedback as they do providing it." ~Alexander Lucia

"Feedback is the breakfast of champions." ~Ken Blanchard

. . . . .

One of the most effective ways of determining the health and success of a company or department is what feedback mechanisms they have in place. Most departments/companies have processes for directing feedback down the career ladder which is very important. It's vital that the front line employees understand what management is looking for from a numbers and performance perspective.

However, that is only half of the story. Great companies and departments have processes in place for feedback to go back up the career ladder, both from the customer and the employees. Your customers and employees are your BEST SOURCE for information on how to continue to improve and succeed. Those that listen to their employees and customers best, typically react quicker to changing market conditions than their competitors, and thus gain the competitive advantage.

To make this effective, two things are needed just like they are when feedback is directed from management to employees. It needs to be structured and action needs to be measured:

Customers

- *Structured* – Consolidate feedback to a meeting or report that is not more frequent than once a week. Any more frequent than that and the feedback loses its impact and just becomes noise. Given the importance, this meeting or report should be headed by the highest ranking member of management possible.
- *Actionable* – Each item mentioned by customers should be assigned to a leader for action. If there was a failure, the remedy should be addressed. If there is an opportunity mentioned, it should be explored. In either case, it is best that there are answers given BEFORE the next week's feedback is discussed. Again, by having the most senior member of management leading this, you ensure better results and accountability.

Employees

- *Structured* – Whether it be quarterly 360 degree feedback, monthly staff brainstorming sessions, or a weekly review of the suggestion box, there needs to be a timeline and a setting.
- *Actionable* – Post your action plan for all to see, and measure your success during the next meeting. These two things will ensure you are held accountable. If you want your 360 degree reviews to have punch, just post them and watch people take them more seriously.

So make sure that you are receiving as much or more feedback than you are giving to stay ahead of the competition, it gives you valuable visibility into your operation, and ultimately ensures success.

LESSON ASSIGNMENT: Ask your staff to fill out a 10 question assessment of your performance on a 1 to 5 scale. Use the 10 questions following, or use your own. Then have them submit them into a box to maintain anonymity. Remember to look at it constructively, and don't get defensive.

1. Does your Supervisor/Manager exhibit leadership qualities in the roles he/she plays in the company?
2. Does your Supervisor/Manager effectively solve problems?
3. Does your Supervisor/Manager have the ability to motivate his/her direct reports?
4. Are your Supervisor/Manager 's work methods and approach to accomplishing his/her job effective, efficient, and continuously improving?
5. Does your Supervisor/Manager have a high attention to detail?
6. Does your Supervisor/Manager prioritize action items and his/her work in general and then follow through on the priorities he/she sets?
7. Does your Supervisor/Manager foster a team environment?
8. Does your Supervisor/Manager manage their time well?
9. Does your Supervisor/Manager multi-task well?
10. How timely is your Supervisor/Manager about the completion of commitments and assignments, in your experience?

Going Outside the Box is GREAT

Diary Entry #25 – June 25th

"If everyone has to think outside the box, maybe it is the box that needs fixing." ~Malcolm Gladwell

"Winners must learn to relish change with the same enthusiasm & energy that we have resisted it in the past." ~Tom Peters

.   .   .   .   .

Want to freshen up the workplace a little? Shake things up? Create a little fun? Big impact often necessitates doing something that breaks down people's expectations. It doesn't mean doing something stupid, but a little crazy isn't always bad, and the benefits of doing so in a structured environment like the workplace can be huge. There are three main benefits that can come out of this:

1. It often recharges and re-energizes your team through the excitement of doing something new and possibly something they aren't entirely comfortable with.
2. Sometimes breaking the routine can reveal new opportunities for your department or the company as it gets the mind working in a different way.

3. By continuing to think "outside the box" and taking action on it, you inspire a culture that accepts and relishes change which is one of the most essential facets of an exceptional organization.

This requires you, and your organization, to be OK with failure and ready to switch back if need be. It is also best if you have the buy in of your team. Many of the ideas and energy that will be generated by this exercise WILL come from line level staff. Honestly, I can't come up with your departments ideas, since they will need to be tailored to you, but I have tried 5 of the 6 below "out of the box" things (just to kick start your thinking):

- Give behind the scenes employees a chance to be customer facing
- Change the hold music or the overhead music
- Start using customers first names instead of "Mr./Mrs"
- Offer a competitor's product as an add-on (possibly blurring the line between crazy and stupid)
- Have managers serve coffee to employees throughout the day
- Do away with a vital piece of equipment (think Apple stores doing away with cash registers)

Not all results will be easily measurable, but you should make every attempt to document the impact:

- What did you learn about your staff?
- What did you learn about the customer?
- What did you learn about the process?
- What did you learn about yourself?

Start small, then gradually try larger and larger out of the box ideas, and don't forget your back-up plan to revert to the "in the box" process if it is apparent you have strayed too far.

Oh yeah, and don't forget to have fun, experimenting and growing an organization should have a little adventure in it.

LESSON ASSIGNMENT: Test one of the above examples this week. Alternatively, you could e-mail your staff and ask for suggestions using the above as examples. Whether it is switching cubes, breaking uniform code, breaking the scripting, etc. the important thing is to break up the "hum-drum" routine that the staff is always experiencing.

No B.S. Accountability

Diary Entry #26 – May 26th

"Some people change their ways when they see the light; others when they feel the heat." ~Caroline Schoeder

"Sometimes when you innovate, you make mistakes. It is best to admit them quickly, and get on with improving your other innovations." ~Steve Jobs

. . . . .

What if we were unable to hide our mistakes from our superiors, peers and subordinates? Would that change our behavior, and by way of that, our performance? I say that it DEFINITELY would. I remember hearing a coworker of mine talking about a football game where a receiver had dropped pass after pass. His comment was that he was sure that player would be putting in extra work the coming week because "It makes a difference when every one of your mistakes is played out on ESPN highlights to a national audience". But hiding our mistakes is far too easy in today's organizations, usually through one or both of the following:

- Doing and reporting nothing – hiding in the shadows of everyone's busy day
- Doing and reporting everything – hiding in plain sight behind a sea of information

The key to tackling both of these is clarity: coming up with just a few black and white metrics or milestones that EVERYONE knows about. It shouldn't be more than three, otherwise you start seeing glazed faces staring back at you. Think back to the analogy of sports again, while there are a lot of things that go into an exceptional performance, athletes are graded on VERY FEW metrics (points scored, turnovers, etc.)

If you oversee staff meetings in your organization try the below format (if your boss runs them, ask him/her to institute a similar format):

1. Have each department head mention what one, two, or three things (metrics or projects) they are working on, and what they are doing between now and the next staff meeting to improve them or move them along.
2. Write out meeting minutes that include the details.
3. During the next staff meeting, go over the results of their work since the last staff meeting. If there are failures, ask what was learned and how they are going to get back on track.
4. During the next staff meeting carry onward.

For your staff it can be as simple as publicly displaying the results of a couple of performance metrics every day. If they know that everyone is going to see their sales figures every day, you may see their behavior change (this one act has helped me innumerable times to improve the performance of my staff on a particular item). It is important that the information is not sensitive, like if their sales have a known effect on their pay or any other factor. But the main thing is to provide that feedback daily.

Psychologists will tell you that between pleasure and pain, people will do more to avoid pain than they will do to seek out pleasure. As long as the culture of your organization supports learning from mistakes (when they are not repeated), the fear of embarrassment could be very useful in driving performance improvements.

LESSON ASSIGNMENT: Start with yourself. There is usually one door leading into or out of your department. Post a sign stating what it is that you will do, when it will be done, and encouraging everyone to ask you about it on that date. Scary thought isn't it? But do you think you'll be more likely to get it done by the due date?

Then take turns with your staff doing the same thing, making a "commitment board" of accomplishments.

Don't Treat People Like Robots

Diary Entry #32 – July 22nd

"Lead and inspire people. Don't try to manage and manipulate people. Inventories can be managed but people must be lead." ~Ross Perot

"Good leaders make people feel that they're at the very heart of things, not at the periphery." ~Warren Bennis

·   ·   ·   ·   ·

While the assembly line created by Henry Ford was a milestone achievement of genius for manufacturing, very little is spoken about the enormous impact physically and mentally on the employees of the time, as well as the high levels of turnover in the plants. While robots have in many places replaced the human element in assembly lines, we still find "standardization" practices in many businesses that reduce the human to robot status. To put it succinctly, this is a mistake.

While Standard Operating Procedures and rigorous guidelines are essential tools for the proper management of the staff, it is too easy and too tempting to let these run amuck. After all, if you simply tell everyone exactly what to do, and expect them to do it, you can take the rest of the week off! But over time, you will begin to see your productivity decrease and turnover increase as your staff becomes increasing bored and frustrated with their work.

Some things to consider:

- *People require different things to make them work* – Machines run solely on fuel, and while money is a decent fuel to use for people, you need to tap into the emotional element to really have them perform. Inspiration, passion and purpose are what separate a great manager from a tolerable one.
- *People need variety in their job* – This was the failing of the assembly line, you could only screw on bumpers so long before you went crazy. Try to mix up their duties on a day to day basis or include them in the occasional project to mix things up. For more frivolous faire, you can throw in special days (pot-lucks, dress-up days, or celebrations) to give them something to look forward to at work and break up the day to day monotony.
- *People are susceptible to outside influence* - They are often affected even by decisions that don't directly affect them. What other employers pay their employees, or what their job duties are. Even what is going on in other industries or departments. You must guard against the "grass is always greener" syndrome to maintain motivation amongst your staff.

There is however one big area where robots and people are similar:

- *People require maintenance too* – Your employees need your attention, they need you to tell them when they do well, and above all, they need continual retraining on new techniques and refreshers on the old ones. So while we don't want to treat our staff like robots, we do not want to neglect preventative and regular maintenance.

Never forget that each and every one of your employees is unique and while it may be easier to fit them all into a nice little mold, you will miss out on the benefit of each of their talents AND you will lead down a path to mediocrity and inferior performance if you do so. So keep working on your policies and procedures, but be careful that you also address the human element in your management.

LESSON ASSIGNMENT: Ask your employees what the three most boring and repetitive tasks are that they do on a regular basis. Not the tasks they like to do least, the ones that are boring and repetitive. Next, ask them what new things they would like to learn and/or where they would like to cross train. From this information you can take action to address the boring tasks and start working on getting them more time on the tasks they do like.

Everyone Won't Agree With Your Changes, Do Them Anyway

Diary Entry #35 – August 7th

"I don't know the key to success, but the key to failure is trying to please everybody." ~ *Bill Cosby*

"Effective leaders help others to understand the necessity of change and to accept a common vision of the desired outcome." ~*John Kotter*

· · · · ·

If you want what you've always got, then keep doing what you've always done. That old saying is only partially true, for the real fact in business is that if you keep doing what you've always done, you'll eventually go extinct. As a manager you must constantly improve your operation if you want to succeed. The interesting/sad part is that a portion of your staff will not be at all interested in the change, no matter how positive it is.

DO NOT let this dissuade you from changing, but you do need to be aware of it so that you can bring along as much of your staff as possible (and make it much easier on yourself in the process). Whenever we go through a change in my department I go through three steps that help me successfully get buy in, AND set us up for success on the next change:

1) **Tackle ignorance** – Most of the time your staff simply has no idea why you do what you do. <u>You need to tell them!!!</u> Explain how the process/change is going to work from start to finish so that they know you have a plan. Most employees want to see the company and department be as successful as possible, and if you explain why the change is in the best interests of everyone, buy-in is easier. Explaining the "why" also addresses your staff's fear of the unknown, which can be a big source of resistance as well.

2) **Respond to feedback** – Nothing goes as planned, but the key to success is dealing with those unplanned events that come up well. One of the big keys is getting immediate feedback from your staff as to what is working and what isn't working, and to act on what they do tell you. This not only helps you manage the change better and make adjustments to fix what isn't working, it also brings your staff into the process and helps establish their ownership of it.

3) **Show them the results** – This should be self-explanatory, but it builds political capital for the next change that you would like to make and gives them a sense of accomplishment. Also, those who were resistant or negative before will have a harder time making their case.

Even with these steps, there will still be people that will not like the change and will be vocal about it. It is important that you do not dismiss them, but try to bring them into the fold. The absolute BEST way to do that? With one question:

"Why don't you think this is a good idea?"

You can then reiterate the "why", show them results if you have them, and gather their feedback to make it better. This still won't win over everyone, but it is an excellent way to get some of the stragglers on board.

LESSON ASSIGNMENT: The next change that you make in the department, big or small, go out and ask for the "Why". Ask your team why the change is important before you give them the answer, this will give you great practice with both positive and negative sides of the change. Then communicate what you believe is the "Why". Based on what your staff has already said, you should be able to address many of their concerns in this communication.

If You Wouldn't Recommend Your Staff, Maybe You Need a New Staff

Diary Entry #41 – August 22nd

"A man must be big enough to admit his mistakes, smart enough to profit from them, and strong enough to correct them." ~John C. Maxwell

"Instead of worrying about what people say of you, why not spend time trying to accomplish something they will admire." ~Dale Carnegie

. . . . .

The question is really whether you are proud enough and satisfied enough with your staff to send them over to someone else's team in a similar role. If you have questions as to whether they would represent you well to you peers and supervisors, then what makes you think they are representing you well now???

Recently I was asked to assist another department, and this thought came to me when I began hand-picking who I would send over and realized there were more than a handful of people I DID NOT want to send over to a peer of mine. Now if I'm not satisfied with how they represent me to someone else inside the company, why would I be satisfied with how they represent me to the customer?

So what I had to do is answer two questions?

1) Why didn't I want to send them to my peer?
   a. Did they not know their job functions well?
   b. Did they display unprofessional behavior?
   c. Was their job performance low?
   d. Did they lack follow-through
   e. Was it something else?
2) What was my plan for addressing the reason I decided upon?

Those people are now receiving extra attention and coaching from the training manager. Receiving extra attention and coaching from their Supervisor. AND extra attention and coaching from me.

We should all have procedures in place to "coach up, or coach out", but these procedures are not, and probably should not, be a failsafe for ensuring you have great people in place. Modern day business requires flexibility and agility. My department is currently being agile in addressing these individuals, time will tell whether there is a need to be flexible in our approach to them.

But by all means, take a look at your staff and ask yourself whether you would have any hesitations about sending ANY of them to a peer of yours. Then DO SOMETHING about that information.

LESSON ASSIGNMENT: Write down the names of each one of your staff members. Now circle the ones you would be happy to "loan" a peer of yours. Those without a circle need some attention and training. The key is to take action on this information, so start with one person without a circle around their name and answer the questions above and put a plan in place to address their shortcomings TODAY.

Managing Negative Small Groups

Diary Entry #43 – August 29th

"The secret of managing is to keep the five guys who hate you away from the four guys who haven't made up their minds." ~Casey Stengel

"Pick battles big enough to matter, small enough to win." -~Jonathan Kozol

.　　.　　.　　.　　.

Two people don't make a vicious circle, they make a vicious line. What you really need to watch out for are groups of three to five. This seems to be the ideal number for a good ole "bitch session". Any more than that and the people lose engagement and run the risk of having more dissenters. Of course, if the group is comprised of employees who do not show an inclination to be troublemakers, there isn't much to worry about either. The vicious circle is powerful because it creates a negative feedback loop that becomes worse and worse with every turn.

The key is doing your job well enough to where there aren't many people that will fall into the feedback loop, or better yet, you develop people who will out and out stop it. But even with that, these circles will inevitably occur. So what to do?

- *Touch on the people who could be in your corner* — Make a mental note to "Say Hi" or "Touch base" with them within the next couple of days of noticing the small group to mitigate any damage.
- *Touch the people who aren't in your corner* — Hopefully to solicit a rethinking of the degree of negativity. Again, say "Hi", ask how they are doing, and see what they are up to.
- *Observe them on an ongoing basis* — To determine whether they are effective, have been turned, or are possibly becoming increasingly negative.
- *Be consistent and persistent* — These sort of demonstrated behaviors usually take time to turn around, so be ready to be working with these employees for the long term. There is rarely a quick turnaround.

The ability to show that you can relate and manage more negative groups can also prove to be especially beneficial in very large organizations. I've seen several people be able to show their prowess as Supervisors and Managers by managing a "difficult" team well that had consistently been difficult to manage by others.

I realize that this seems completely paranoid on a certain level, but when you manage a large group, it is often the subtle things that you notice and take action on that are preventative against something larger coming in to play. Even if you are a great manager, you won't be able to please everyone, and you need to be aware of them and manage them appropriately.

The one caution I have regarding this is that you do not want to "reward" complainers with overly excessive attention. This can easily become a show of favoritism if not worked in with a regular show of attention to your entire staff.

LESSON ASSIGNMENT: Choose the three people that you need to reach out to over the next week that you are not sure are on your side, then reach out to them. Say "Hi", ask them how their weekend was, or if they have anything planned for the weekend, anything to get a conversation going.

Aces in Places

Diary Entry #47 – September 12th

"Everybody is a genius. But if you judge a fish by its ability to climb a tree, it will live its whole life believing that it is stupid." ~*Albert Einstein*

"The task of leadership is not to put greatness into humanity, but to elicit it, for the greatness is already there." ~*John Buchan*

. . . . .

The best companies get the most out of their operations by leveraging their assets to the maximum. Your asset with the most upside is your staff, and the best way to leverage them is to have the right people in the right places, "Aces in Places" if you will. So how do you do it?

- **Who do you have** – First you need to assess your staff and determine what they are good at, what they think they are good at, and what they would like to do. You need to do all three, to check for aptitude, confidence and motivation respectively, and to get the broadest list of current and potential "Aces".
- **Where are your problems** – If you don't know where your problems and opportunities are, then check with your boss (though he/she may rightfully tell you that you should

already know where they lie). But just as important is knowing who on your team matches up against problems and opportunities that come up along the way. Make a short list of issues/opportunities next to the list of your staff's assessment.

- **How to fix it** – Full utilization of your team is essential and they must have proper direction on how to fix what they are tasked with. Give clear direction, match with mentors, create specialized teams, but whatever you do, continue to manage the process.

Every single employee in the company has a strength that can be leveraged for the benefit of everyone. Those who discover those strengths in their employees and then use them in the exact spot that leverages that talent to its full extent will be the companies and departments who lead us all forward.

Now I am not recommending just leaving them in their area of strength, but by recognizing their strength you can use them when necessary, and as a means to set the bar for what maximum performance in that particular area may look like.

LESSON ASSIGNMENT: Take three random employees and find their biggest area of strength. Then one day next week, put them in that area of strength for the entire day and see what happens. This may not be anything permanent, maybe you do it only once a week or only in emergencies, but you try it out and see what you can learn.

Cut the BS, Make Policies Relevant

Diary Entry #33 – July 29th

"Almost all quality improvement comes via simplification of design, manufacturing... layout, processes, and procedures." ~Tom Peters

"Never tell people how to do things. Tell them what to do and they will surprise you with their ingenuity." ~General George Patton

. . . . .

I'm not a lawyer, and barring something unforeseen, neither are your employees (full disclosure, I once had an ex-lawyer as an employee). So why is your Policy and Procedure Manual and/or Standard Operating Procedures written like legislation going in front of Congress? If you want to get the benefit of an instruction manual or a policy, it needs to be written in a way that speaks to the audience, in this case your employees. I recommend three basic guidelines when I'm tasking someone with policy or procedure writing:

1. **Give them the "Why"** – The most important thing is conveying the purpose of a policy or procedure. Your policies are like a framed painting in the museum. The frame is the boundaries you have put in place, the step by step, rules, etc. But the "why" is the painting itself. If you don't

explain the "why", then you have no substance, and the intent is too easily lost. The "why" gives the policy or procedure its importance. This also eliminates those employees who follow the "letter of the law, but not the intent".

2. **Less is more** – Learn to live within the flexibility. If you explain the "why", then you do not need to exhaustively explain every single permutation and scenario that can possibly come to pass (I once had a dress code policy with the pictures of 50 women's sandals that told which were acceptable and which weren't). Also, your audience has a finite attention span, so leave out the extras and stick to the most important points. Nothing is as useless as a 2,000 page manual on how to do a job.

3. **Help them find what they want** – No more than three clicks or page turns away. If you must print it off for everyone, spend the extra dollar to have it tabbed/paginated correctly. If your staff can't find what they need quickly, then these policies and procedures are basically useless. Yes, you will go over it in new hire training, but it should also be a reference, and for that reason it needs to be easily navigable.

Legal writing often buries things deeply in a web of irrelevant and "big worded" nonsense. Be careful as a manager to ensure that your policies and procedures serve their purpose of informing and directing the behavior of your employees. Too often they are used to limit liability, or to sound impressive to a VP or HR department head. Great leaders serve their staff, and keep their needs at the forefront.

LESSON ASSIGNMENT: Go to your Training Manual and/or your Standard Operating Procedures, and for the ten most commonly used functions, add at the very beginning of the procedure "Why is this important: _____". The "why" can be to reduce errors, to ensure you are protected from legal liability, to increase cross-selling, to establish a professional environment, etc. but the most important thing is explaining why it deserves their attention. The better your "why" the better the policy will be.

Calling Out Mistakes

Diary Entry #51 – September 25th

"I always try to go hard on the issue and soft on the person." ~ *Henry Cloud*

"The man who does things makes many mistakes, but he never makes the biggest mistake of all - doing nothing." ~*Ben Franklin*

.   .   .   .   .

There is a big difference between calling out a mistake to kick your employee's butt into gear, and kicking it so hard that they never want to come out and play anymore. What you are looking for is an environment of accountability and issue solving. Too often the punishment is too harsh, leading to your staff wasting time trying to hide mistakes instead of fixing them. It also leads to an overall environment of fear, and senior management being kept in the dark about issues instead of being able to address them.

So how do you stay firm about expectations and performance, yet still instill an environment of openness:

- *Clear expectations* – Let them know when you ask for something or start an initiative what the timeline is and the expectations. Write it down in a place where you can come back to it (meeting requests are a great place to do that). This helps with accountability when done <u>consistently</u>.
- *Get all of the info BEFORE you fly off of the handle* – Ensure that you are directing your ire at the right person. Too often we are so prepared to issue discipline that we cut our employees off, only to find out later, we misdirected our focus.
- *Don't just identify the mistakes, HELP with the solution (even if it is just offering your support)* – It's important to get back on track so that the employee can be focused on productivity instead of dwelling on the failure. It also reassures them that you still have faith in them to complete/fix what they started.
- *Ensure that the penalty for hiding a mistake is MUCH worse than bringing it forward* – This is essential and one of the few times I recommend going hard on someone. It is imperative that issues are brought forward so that the entire team can address them before they become a bigger issue.
- *Don't accept excuses (but don't ignore them, there is often some truth about an obstacle in them)* - Remember that you pay your people to anticipate problems, so usually they should see it coming and they should adjust or ask for assistance before it becomes a larger issue.

There are plenty of times where you need to be VERY firm (repeated mistakes, safety issues, legal violations, etc), but it is important that you do not create an environment where nobody is allowed to make a mistake, because the best way to avoid mistakes is TO DO NOTHING. And that is a recipe for your business going out of business!

LESSON ASSIGNMENT: The next time that someone makes a mistake, bring them into your office and ask them:

- What they can learn from this?

- What can WE do to solve it?
- Can we roll anything out to the staff to prevent them from making the mistake?

Then give them the project of rolling out the new training or awareness campaign to address the issue. This turns their failure into a productive project and creates a sense of ownership.

Excellence Expected or Mediocrity Tolerated

Diary Entry #52 – September 26th

"Be a yardstick of quality. Some people aren't used to an environment where excellence is expected." ~Steve Jobs

"The best performers across every field have an unwavering desire for excellence for what they do, the way they think, and the way they work." ~Jim Collins

. . . . .

Do you have an environment in your department where excellence is the expectation of every single employee, or do you have an environment where the mediocre employees continue to plod along in a continuous march of blandness? While companies who tolerate mediocrity can compete with other companies who tolerate mediocrity, they are generally CRUSHED by companies who expect excellence. So since you do not yet run the company, how can you set an expectation of excellence in your department for success?

- **Get clear on Metrics** – It is IMPERATIVE that you find a way to measure performance that is black and white, and that you communicate those metrics to each employee regularly. One on one meetings between supervisors and line-level employees are essential, but these metrics should be displayed and/or communicated daily and publicly as well to really drive home their importance and therefore the accountability of the employee.

- **Set the bar "reasonably" high before you raise it higher** – Excellence is just that, excellent. So you do not want to celebrate a mediocre performance. With that said, if you have a culture of mediocrity, then you need to build momentum. The 1st win begets the 2nd win, then 3rd, then success becomes an expectation
- **Give constant feedback** – A staff that is achieving excellence wants to know what is going on constantly. Feedback will be the fuel that powers the racecar, so get ready to give it as quickly as you can. Daily is better than weekly, hourly is better than daily, etc. Feedback should not just center on results, but involve coaching on how to improve those results.
- **Be consistent** – Most everything takes longer than we want it to take. So whatever timeline you want....triple it, and if you are persistent, that will secure success.

The idea is that great performers are rewarded and recognized, and poor performers understand that excellence is expected and they cannot hide (they shape up or ship out). It is in this environment that greatness begins to flower.

LESSON ASSIGNMENT: Take your latest focus (customer service, sales, expenses, cross-sales, etc) and put the four elements above into place. Once you have worked through and seen the improvement, work on another, then another. As with most things, don't try to focus on more than three things at a time or you will lose the impact.

Water The Garden Every Day

Diary Entry for Book #1

"A leader is not an administrator who loves to run others, but one who carries water for his people so that they can get on with their jobs" ~Robert Townsend

"Tell me and I forget. Teach me and I remember. Involve me and I learn." ~ Benjamin Franklin

. . . . .

Every day you are not in your garden, weeds begin to grow. They could be negativity/gossip, they could be improper procedures, or just about anything. What is key is that you spend time tending it.

First Step – Noticing

A good gardener patrols his/her garden to check on its progress and state as often as possible. Similar to this, you should walk around and notice things. If you have a staff of 10 or less, you should speak with them, at least briefly, every day (preferably multiple times every day). If you have a staff under 50, you should speak with everyone once a week. It can be a short "how are you doing", "How was the weekend", "Any plans for the weekend" etc. which can lead into longer topics or not. The key is that you begin this process so that you can establish a relationship, and so that you can notice strengths, weaknesses, and any changes.

Second Step – Watering, Feeding, and Maintenance

A good gardener is always careful to water and feed his/her garden and do any pruning or weeding on a regular basis. Like the gardener, you should be gathering and dispensing feedback (both positive and negative) on a regular basis. But as with tending a garden, you must do just the right amount of feedback giving (you can't over or under water, just like you need to strike the right balance of positive and negative feedback). You are also able to deal with any problems (weeds) that pop up, and do any pruning (skillset coaching) during this stage as well.

Third Step – Harvest and Prep for Next Year

A gardener is careful to get the most out of the harvest, and just as careful about preparing for future crops. Just like the gardener, at this stage you look to make those small tweaks to get the best performance out of your staff, as time has gone on, and you have continued to speak with them regularly, you should be able to make small suggestions to maximize their performance. Likewise, you begin to lay the groundwork for career development to ensure their impact on the operation is a long and healthy one.

While I went a little crazy with the analogy, it is one that is important. As a great Supervisor or Manager, you must be out tending to your greatest assets, your people. You cannot be successful without their effort, and by way of that, you serve them like a gardener serves his plants.

LESSON ASSIGNMENT: Go on a talking binge. Regardless of the size of your staff, speak with every one of your employees each day for a week. Ask them about work, ask them about what their pet peeves are at work, talk about sports/movies, anything to get you interacting. The first step as mentioned above is noticing, so begin noticing things. Once you've done that, you can begin giving feedback as well on what you observe.

When It Comes To Compassion, Just Do It

Diary Entry for Book #2

"The simple act of paying positive attention to people has a great deal to do with productivity" ~Tom Peters

"If you're good to your staff when things are going well, they'll rally when times go bad." ~Mary Kay Ash

. . . . .

One of the strangest things I have come across in my career is the tendency to second guess whether you should show some human compassion towards a staff member or give them a pat on the back. I've experienced it in my own career as a manager, and I truly believe I could have been better if I had just followed the rule in the title above....Just do it.

Your department is made up of human beings. Of mothers, sons, daughters, fathers. Finding ways to show our staff that we care and appreciate them, and finding ways to positively reinforce behavior is one of the cornerstones of any great management strategy. Study after study says that you need a two to one or even four to one positive feedback to negative feedback ratio to maintain a "positive workplace". Finding that much positive is often difficult in the prevalent corporate culture of "addressing the problem" that we find ourselves in today. So why don't we take advantage of the human side of compassion to add to our positive/negative ratio? The concerns from the management side are generally as follows:

1. Are you being fair, showing favorites?
2. Will it lead to a time consuming situation? I've got a report due at 4pm.
3. Will it diminish any negative feedback you have in the future?
4. Does it cross a personal life/professional life line?

But the fact is, you are either in control of the outcome of the above concerns (#1, #2, #4), or the concern itself is misplaced (#3, those I have a closer relationship with are more apt to pay attention to my feedback and want to do well for me).

Now there are a few rules/guidelines to consider when treading into these waters:

- *Be respectful* – Remember, you are the boss, and you set the tone for your engagement. If you act respectful and "normal" during the course of the interaction, everyone else will consider it normal as well.
- *Keep it in the workplace* – Never offer to go get a cup of coffee down at Starbucks and talk about it. If you need privacy, go to your office or a conference room.
- *Control the time* – If it starts running long, take 30 seconds to say your final piece/thoughts, then excuse yourself to head back to work.

So send the e-mail, have the conversation, give them a smile, show your staff that you are paying attention and that you care about them and they will move mountains for you. We all spend half of our waking hours at work, so let's set a caring tone. What you should be looking for is excuses to show them compassion, not excuses to not show them compassion.

LESSON ASSIGNMENT: Begin listening for personal events in your employees lives (illnesses, kids birthdays, sporting events, milestones, etc). These can be overheard by you through the employee themselves or their coworkers or relayed to you by Leads and/or Supervisors. Put a note on your calendar and begin following up with the employee directly, there's really no other way than to dive right in.

Great Talent:
Hard To Find & Tough To Develop

.

Stop! You're Hiring The Wrong People

Diary Entry #13 – May 14th

"Hire character. Train skill." ~Peter Schutz

"But how can I get experience until I get a job that gives me experience?"
~Michael J. Fox – The Secret of my Success

. . . . .

Too many managers are looking for the wrong thing when they sit across the table from a prospective employee. Which would you rather have for the next one to five years? An average employee who can start right away, or a fantastic employee who will take a month of tutoring? I know, I'm phrasing it in a way that is leading, but it illustrates the shortsightedness of the "skill" approach. I'd rather trade a dozen headaches down the road for just one headache today.

Barring an absolute need for advanced schooling or training, I can teach anybody to do anything, and I'd be willing to bet that you can too (I've got faith). Oftentimes I will see a resume cross my desk with years and years of applicable work experience, but this can be a detriment just as much as a positive if they do not come from an operation that mirrors mine. Furthermore, you are often limiting yourself to someone without the capacity to contribute more to your company (through upward advancement). If they've been in the same position for a number of years it can mean negative things just as well as positive.

One of the primary reasons that managers take the short-term view on hiring is that they have a desperate need to fill a position as soon as possible. They have work that needs to be done due to either business growth, or more common, someone leaving the company. While this gets into contingency planning a little, there are two ways to ease the pain in the future:

- *Structured training in a live environment* – If you have a need to have someone "hit the ground running", then structure your training to bring them up to speed on certain tasks that they can get real world practice in that will take part of the load off of your existing staff right away.
- *Cross-training* – Do you have Admins that can handle some of the tasks from the prior bullet point? What about people in other departments? A little help for a couple of weeks may be all it takes to get someone up to speed.

If you put these two things in place prior to needing to hire someone, you may be able to fend off the chorus of peers and superiors who want you to bring someone in immediately.

So given that you have cleared the way for this person, what should we be looking for? For me, I'm looking for people who can solve problems (capacity to think/learn), have a generally positive outlook (capacity to deal with failure), and who can get passionate about something (capacity to be a product evangelist). For you, it may be something else, but your interviews should lead you to an assessment of what character traits or "capacities" are important to you. Some of the questions I often use:

- If you could change one thing about the operation of your former/current employer, what would it be?
- What was your favorite thing about your last job?
    - What didn't you like?
- What was the biggest challenge you faced on a daily basis?
    - How did you deal with it?

Can they think outside of the box? What gets them excited about work? And how do they deal with challenges? These are the most important issues we should be looking for in a prospective employee.

This isn't to say that I do not value skills and work experience, but they are a secondary evaluator, not the primary trigger. I want people who think and can grow, so that's what I go after. I'd like to think you should too.

LESSON ASSIGNMENT: The next time you are conducting hiring, broaden your pool of candidates by taking out the "relevant work experience required", then look to interview twice as many candidates as you did the last time. Look for potential, not immediate impact. During my latest round of hiring, I interviewed 12 people for every one that I hired (we hired three). Take your time, and only settle for the best, it is without a doubt the most important thing you will do for your department and your company.

Importance of a Diverse Staff

Diary Entry #22 – June 5ᵗʰ

"None of us are as smart as all of us." ~*Japanese Proverb*

"When spider webs unite, they can tie up a lion." ~*Ethiopian Proverb*

.   .   .   .   .

Having people with the same background, experience, and talent is a recipe for eventual failure. Yes, you need the ability to do the job, but one of the magic ingredients to any business or department is diversity. If we have diversity, we have the ability to share ourselves and our experiences with the whole operation to lift everyone and everything up. It is like having your own in house consultants that can advise you on best practices in different areas:

- "When this happened at my last job, we did _____, and it worked great"
- "Every month, we did _____, and it reduced expenses and improved revenue 10%"
- "What you need is a report we used to call _____, that would do the trick"

The challenges you face in running your department are rarely unique. Leveraging the prior experience of your staff helps you to more quickly solve those problems. It's a responsible use of your diverse talent.

Diversity of background can also help mitigate the squabbling between departments. If you have someone who worked in that department (Marketing, Sales, Accounting, Legal, etc) they can provide valuable perspective that can cut down negativity before it even starts. You don't know what the other guy is going through until you've been there yourself. When there are concerns about another department, go to your in-house people with experience in that area and ask them what may be going on. You'll probably save yourself some headaches in the process.

Similar to the above, the last area where diversity can help is understanding different customers and employees. Again, the key is to engage your staff in order to leverage their experience for the understanding of everybody.

Now I'm not saying that you should only start looking for people outside of your company, or with backgrounds you don't currently have on your roster. Promotion or hiring from within is how you reward excellence and develop talent. What I'm saying is that the diversity of your workforce may be a strategic advantage that is not being used to its full extent now. There may be a hidden jewel of knowledge just waiting to be uncovered by the right situation.

So how do we start putting this into practice? What I recommend is the following:

- Ask your staff to submit the one best tool/skill that they have seen put into use in their prior work history.
- Find out what your staff (or even peer's) backgrounds are.

Who knows, you may be pleasantly surprised at what you find, and discover the path to an even stronger and more successful organization.

LESSON ASSIGNMENT: In addition to the above, make a list of your employees, and next to each of their names put down their last three jobs, and their three biggest strengths. This creates a reference for you to engage them when you either need a team to tackle an issue, or need to look for new ideas.

When Hiring: Take the Ferrari over the Honda

Diary Entry #36 – August 8th

"Endeavors succeed or fail because of the people involved. Only by attracting the best people will you accomplish great deeds." ~Colin Powell

"Get the best people and train them well." ~Scott McNealy

. . . . .

Recently I was conducting interviews for a new position we were creating within the department. As I went through the interviews, one of the candidates showed a huge upside well beyond what the position entailed. So much so, that we would honestly look to adjust the scope of the position, and would probably need to in order to keep the candidate's interest over the months and years in this position. I also had a number of candidates that were perfect fits for the position, would be satisfied with it, would excel, and wouldn't need any extra coaching.

But one thing I thought of in the interview was that I was being offered the services of a Ferrari, for work that only required a Honda at basically no additional cost. The only additional cost I

73

would bear would be the time and effort needed to keep that person interested, the maintenance if you will, on my new Ferrari.

This has happened more and more as we have come out of the recession. There are a number of candidates for positions that are over-qualified. There are some who dismiss these candidates right away, and I can't necessarily fault them, even though I am one who is apt to hire them right away. There are a couple of things I always keep in mind before I bring them on board though:

- **Why do they want the position** – I am always very upfront in the interview and ask them directly why they are looking at a job that they are certainly overqualified for. It's important to know whether the work will be at all interesting to them, or whether they will be bored, and therefore, unproductive. It also gives you an idea if they will be leaving as soon as something better comes along. An important consideration when looking to bring on one of these candidates.
- **How much time/effort am I willing to put in to encourage them** – Superstars are just as needy as your poor performers, and often much more so. I need to have the time in my schedule to give them more support, or be willing to expend the department's resources on them. As with the example above with the cars, there may not be any extra financial cost, but the maintenance costs could kill you.

I'm willing to generally take on people who are overqualified because I have a belief that they will elevate their peers, and thus the department. However, I am not naïve in thinking they may leave soon, or that I will need to give them more TLC than the average employee. But I think that is a small price to pay for the upgrade, so I say take the Ferrari!

LESSON ASSIGNMENT: The next time you are looking to hire a new employee, do not dismiss those who appear to be vastly overqualified. Instead, invite them into an interview and ask them why they are interested and how they think their experience can help the operation. You may very well be thrilled with their response.

Uncover the Talent that is Right In Front of You

Diary Entry #45 – September 5th

"The task of the leader is to get his people from where they are to where they have not been." ~Henry Kissinger

"Leaders take people where they want to go. Great leaders take people where they don't necessarily want to go, but ought to be." ~Jimmy Carter

.   .   .   .   .

Too much of the time our support team toils in obscurity. Your IT Helpdesk personnel are cogs in the machine, usually they get no outward recognition, their boss does. Your frontline sales staff has a few people who are LEAPS AND BOUNDS above everyone else, but are not heard outside their own operation.

If you are serious about tapping the potential of your company's staff (and I trust that you are) you MUST tap into the best of your frontline crew. We've talked before about bringing them into the operation from a feedback perspective, as your staff often has the best ideas about improvements to the operation because they are in the trenches. But if you want to kick that process into high gear, AND help develop the next round of superstar managers in your company, try the following (and please remember we are attempting to do this with hourly front line employees):

- *Exposure* – Give them a project, bring them to the meeting, and develop ways to tap their ideas in a public way. This encourages them to continue to excel, and helps you see if they have what it takes to rise to the next rung in the career ladder.
- *Develop* – Once you've determined that it is worthwhile to continue the exposure, it's time to double down on your efforts. One-on-ones, imparting your wisdom, but taking some wisdom from them in turn (one of the best things you can do). Now is where you try to invest in the employee so that the organization can tap their true potential and really improve overall performance.
- *Assist* – The first success is the most important as it is WAY too easy to get demoralized in the beginning, especially if you feel you are "out of your depth" like an hourly employee may feel they are. So you need to either: help them be successful by whatever means you can, or see to it that they understand that their contribution led to a success in some small way. No matter what, they need to log a win.

Once you have done this a few times within your department, roll it out to some of your peers so they can identify and leverage their best employees. Then bring them all together. The group you have in front of you will most likely be the future of the company.

LESSON ASSIGNMENT: For each project that you are brought in on or tasked with, ask for a volunteer to assist you from amongst your frontline staff. Bring this person to meetings, give them a small assignment, and make sure they share the credit.

One Question that Tells You if You Are a Great Leader

Diary Entry #42 – August 24th

"If you think you're leading and no one is following you, then you're only taking a walk." ~Afghan Proverb

"One measure of leadership is the caliber of people who choose to follow you." ~Dennis A. Peer

. . . . .

Do you want a great questions that tells you where you are as a leader?

If you were to jump ship to another company, who on your staff would join you in a lateral move?

As you move up the ranks of companies, your success relies in greater and greater amounts on the efforts of your staff. Great staff equals greater performance by your team, and thus further rockets your career forward. Being able to bring along a great team is essential to any high-performing manager. As I look back over the career of great leaders, they have more often than not had a team of people who followed them everywhere, and provided them with phenomenal support. So what else does the question tell us? The most obvious is which areas of your department you are serving:

- Would any of your leads move with you?
- Is there a certain area of your operation where nobody would follow?
- Or is there an area of your operation where everyone would follow?

The answers to these questions tell you where you need to focus your time and energy, and where you may have spent too much time and effort. Your staff craves leadership, and WILL follow it elsewhere, whether that is with you or someone else. So what is your staff looking for:

"What's in it for me" (WIIFM)

- Are you listening to them, then ACTING on what they are saying? People want to be heard, and want to have a measure of control over their livelihood. Listening and acting is the key.
- Are you helping them do their job better, removing obstacles, and bettering their tools? What have you done recently in this area?
- Are you developing them? Do you have a career path in place, are you helping them individually reach their goals, do you have a succession plan? Who have you moved onward and upward recently?

If you find that there are areas within your department where nobody/everybody would follow you, then you have an imbalance that most likely needs to be addressed. So get to it!

LESSON ASSIGNMENT: Make the list of your employees that you think would follow you to another employer. Look to see if there are certain physical areas or functional areas within your department that show up more or less? Then address the deficient areas.

P.S. That number of people you came up with when you answered the question .... cut that number in half (we tend to overestimate our greatness).

Great Companies Hire **AND RETAIN** Great People

Diary Entry for Book #3

"The growth and development of people is the highest calling of leadership."
~Harvey S. Firestone

"Before you are a leader, success is all about growing yourself. When you become a leader, success is all about growing others." ~Jack Welch

. . . . .

We talk a lot about hiring the right people, but what about keeping the ones you already have? Once you hire them, and then develop them, do you have a plan for retaining them? If you don't, don't worry, you're in the company of most departments and businesses. Your staff is your number one asset, and you need to have a plan for retaining the investment you have made in bringing them on board and developing them.

Great employees are a luxury and need to be tended to. I want you to keep two things in mind:

1. **Great employees want to be challenged and fulfilled in their work**

2. Great employees have options when it comes to where they work.

If you are lucky enough to hire and/or develop a high performing employee, you need to give them more than just a list of daily tasks. You need to give them a vision and a plan for their development. What does that look like?

- *Their Interests*: What interests them about the company, what are they curious about, where would they like to go next in their career?
- *Training*: Have they learned and mastered everything within their current role? If not, this may be the first opportunity for further training. What other applications will develop them (Excel classes, trade application classes, etc). If you invest in them, they will be more interested in making a further investment in the company.
- *Exposure*: They want to be a Supervisor, let them be a relief Supervisor the next time you have a meeting. They want to work in PR, find a way to get them to shadow with the PR department. The key is to provide them insight into all that goes on around them.
- *Expanded Duties*: Once they have had some exposure to further roles and responsibilities, then actually GIVE them some responsibility in that area.

If this sounds like a typical employee development plan, you are mostly correct, but employee development plans are far too rare. Great employees, the ones who really deliver value, typically want more for their careers, and if they don't want to be promoted (many for work/life balance reasons do not), they at a bare minimum would like more control over their work environment.

Now why did I mention that your best employees have options? Well, partly it was to scare you a little in that if you don't work with them you risk losing them (imagine losing 3 of your best 5 employees). But I also mentioned it to highlight some non-personal things that effect their fulfillment in their work.

- *Their work matters*: Have you told your staff how central what they do is to the overall success of the company? Have you explained how their work ties into the vision of the department/company? Tie what they do to something bigger than their day in/day out tasks.
- *The culture is one of excellence*: Challenging some employees and letting the others coast is a recipe for disaster. What you need to do is leverage the challenges you are making with your best, to push everyone in the department. In most instances, pushing the staff forward will result in some turnover because mediocre people don't like an environment of excellence, they want to coast, not learn new things, and thus they need to go, lest they drag everyone down.
- *It's bigger than the department*: When was the last time you gave to the community at large, whether it be time, money, canned goods, etc? If it hasn't happened in a while, you need to look into getting something into action. One of the biggest satisfiers for many employees is community impact.

The above three environmental factors are the more global satisfiers for high performers that keep them around and engaged, don't let them slide.

Your follow through on all of these items is what will be essential to the successful implementation of any employee retention plan, as it is by nature a long term process. If you find your best and brightest leaving for greener pastures (outside the walls of your company), then you'll know that you have some work to do in this area.

LESSON ASSIGNMENT: Go back through your records and determine what your turnover percentage is over the last year (number of people who have left divided by the total number of people in the department). Now if you are a part of a large company, there may be positive turnover where people were promoted into different departments. Track this separately if this is the case. The goal is to minimize negative turnover and increase positive turnover. This provides the base number from which you can track your improvement.

Now ask your staff in a questionnaire the three things they would like to learn/do for their own career development. If you have read prior chapters, you may have this already. Use this to focus your efforts and begin challenging your staff.

The eventual goal is to have an Employee Investment Plan that lays out the different options for them in training and exposure to make their career a long one in your department and company.

Yourself:
If You Can't Mange Yourself, You're In Trouble

Find The Work You Need To Do

Diary Entry #2 – April 28th

"Things which matter most must never be at the mercy of things which matter least." ~Johann Wolfgang von Goethe

"However beautiful the strategy, you should occasionally look at the results." ~Winston Churchill

. . . . .

Too often as managers we look for the work we want to do, or like to do, at the expense of the work we NEED to do. We feel good about this because we are keeping ourselves busy, but that isn't the point is it? This results in not only less productivity, because we are focused on the little things instead of the big things, but also increases the stress on the job as the clouds of what needs to happen (or poor results of delaying what should be done) build. So why do we find ourselves in a position where we are not doing the work we need to do?

- We're not delegating
    - You're doing the work your supervisor should do
    - You're doing the work of the line level staff
    - You're doing the easy work

- We're procrastinating on things we don't want to do
  - Things we've never done before
  - Time intensive tasks
  - Tasks/Projects that involve some risk
- Paralysis by Analysis

To the first two items, I'd say that the delegation topic has been covered at length in any number of places, and not doing something because you don't want to is pretty self-explanatory. What I'm more interested in talking about at a little more length is when you get caught up strategizing and laying out a "grand plan", when simply getting to work will do the trick. Basically you're planning, not doing.

This gets back to "talk less, act more" line of management. What is the first thing we tend to do when there is an issue that needs to be addressed: We call a meeting? We put together a project plan? We put together a focus group? We come up with excuses? All of these (even the last) can be productive, and in most cases should be done at some point. But too often they are a means of delaying taking action.

Meetings, planning, and focus groups can be fun and very interesting, too often because there is little accountability, delayed accountability, or it is something we feel "Executives" do that speaks to our vanity. Not because there is a tangible improvement in the business. How much more powerful would be swift action? You are the manager of the department for goodness sake!!! If someone says sales need to increase, or costs need to be cut, or there is a problem with guest satisfaction, I'd be willing to bet my bottom dollar you have an idea what to do to address it RIGHT NOW. A way that has minimal risk and gets you on the path to success. You don't need to come up with a fancy PowerPoint presentation, work some Gantt Charts, or pull together a brainstorming session. Don't delay it because it'll require more immediate work, don't delay it because it is risky, or it is boring and you've done it before (or it is just "grunt work"), just get it going.

Getting results quickly is what great managers do.

LESSON ASSIGNMENT: Write down the most important task that you have that would improve the company bottom line. Your day isn't a success until that one item is complete, or at least in practical, real world progress (i.e. in action with your staff). I could say more, but isn't "less talk, more action" kind of the idea?

Finding The Subtext

Diary Entry #3 – April 29th

"You can see a lot by looking" ~*Yogi Berra*

"Things don't change, only the way you look at them." ~*Carlos Castaneda*

.   .   .   .   .

One of the biggest differentiators between good managers and great managers is that great managers see things more clearly, and can see further into the future to what is coming towards them and their department. Much of this comes from experience, but I insist that most of it comes from just looking past the surface and asking yourself questions:

- Why is something happening?
- What is the next logical thing to occur?
- How does this affect other things?

It isn't some magical blend of schooling, experience and the right mentor, it is simply doing the work to ask the next question. As you practice this, it becomes easier and quicker and allows you to begin to control the outcomes and future better (or at least guide/prepare it a little). It doesn't mean that you shouldn't take things at face value, and it doesn't mean that you question everything, but you should be listening to that intuition you are working on:

- When someone comes to you with an inter-personal problem with another employee
    - Is it really them that has the problem? Is it ageism, racism, or just being a drama queen by either party? Is this something that could blow up into a larger issue if the two people are vocal in the department?
- A vendor comes to you with a proposed change to a contract
    - Why the change? Is the vendor going to try to squeeze you more? Are they having financial problems?
- Your boss comes to you with a new policy or procedure
    - If they are instituting this, what else makes sense to institute (what now clashes with the policy)? Why did they institute the policy?

As you can see, by asking the questions you can find clarity in the situation, and once you have that, you can "manage" the situation and your department much better. And again, practice, practice, practice reduces the burden and helps prevent you from questioning everything. Here's one last example I know that you have experienced yourself:

You know when one of your peers or employees is having a bad day. Ask them why? You may be surprised at the answer.

LESSON ASSIGNMENT: Write down the last three problems you had to deal with, whether they were people related, product related, or process related. Now write down what caused the problem to occur. Now write down what caused THAT to occur. Now go out and fix that thing. Once you do this more and more you can fix the next thing, then the next, then the next, until you get to the true root of the issue. That's the way to keep things from coming back up.

Excellence is a Habit

Diary Entry #6 – May 5th

"We are what we repeatedly do. Excellence, then, is not an act, but a habit." ~*Aristotle*

"Excellence is not an accomplishment. It is a spirit, a never-ending process." ~ *Lawrence M. Miller*

.   .   .   .   .

There are a number of ways that we use to try to carve out more time in our busy days to work on those REALLY important things. Some of them are good: delegating, prioritizing, using the 80/20 rule, etc. But what I wanted to talk about is one that I have succumbed to far too often in my past: half-assing the minorly important items.

Excellence in all areas of your business can be a HUGE competitive advantage in today's marketplace. But for your company/department, it starts with you, and the tone that you set.

Doing something well takes time. Even when using the maxim "80% of the work is done through 20% of the effort", you still need to find time and focus for that 20%. I use the quote above, because excellence truly is a habit, and once something becomes a habit, it is generally quicker and easier. So how do I turn my instinct to either half-ass something, or even worse, not do something at all into a drive to do everything well?

- *Focus* – Don't leave yourself any "outs", if you don't have time to do it well, focus HARDER. Or plan to do it in two stages, but do not allow yourself to reschedule the second stage at all. Only one scope creep is allowed.
- *I use my gut instinct to prioritize* – If something feels important when I receive it, I JUST DO IT. I don't focus on prioritizing every single item in its perfect slot on my to-do list. If something "feels" important, I tackle it.
- *Leverage the "good" ways to carve out time listed above whenever possible* – The more effective you are at that, the more time you will have to practice excellence.

If you want to stand out, if you really want to set the example for your staff, be excellent all of the time. Creating a habit of excellence does not mean a habit part of the time, it means all of the time.

As I often say, "If it was easy, they wouldn't need us". Time management is only worthwhile if the work you produce is excellent, and excellence takes effort, anybody who tells you otherwise is selling something.

LESSON ASSIGNMENT: Pick three small/insignificant tasks you have every day or week that you just quickly get out of the way. Now do them REALLY well, like you were presenting them to the VP (make the spreadsheet pretty, send out notifications of progress, etc). Get in the habit of doing more of these little tasks like this and watch it become easier.

Embrace What You Don't Know

Diary Entry #12 – May 13th

"An organization's ability to learn, and translate that learning into action rapidly, is the ultimate competitive advantage." ~Jack Welch

"Leaders are more powerful role models when they learn than when they teach" ~Rosabeth Moss Kantor

· · · · ·

Too often we fear and avoid what we don't understand/know. This can be a catastrophic problem for your business career if it becomes persistent. A changing marketplace requires reinvention on a regular basis and that requires you to LEARN new ways to conduct your business. The most successful people have a tendency to be the most curious about things they don't know. They move fast when new opportunities present themselves and through working their "learning" muscle, it becomes easier for them to embrace new ideas, systems, and policies. This increases their skillsets and their knowledge of the operation. As the manager, it is your responsibility to embrace what you don't know about several things:

What your staff duties are: Ideally you would always have an understanding of enough depth to be able to simply step into your staff's role. This gives you an understanding of what they encounter on a daily basis, what struggles they have, and where there may be opportunities. If you came up through the ranks, it's easy and simply needs maintenance as policies, systems and procedures evolve. But if you came in through another department, you may not have this level of familiarity. You must conquer your fear of failure in front your staff and learn what they do. What you don't know (your staff's duties) will be essential to you managing. Too often the incoming manager is too busy to invest the time in training, and prefers to manage from his/her office through spreadsheets and "vision". But without learning what he/she doesn't know, this will only result in marginalized improvement.

The latest "toys" available in your industry: The opposite side of the coin from your needs is what is available to your department. Those who stay abreast of the changes in their industry can easily match needs with solutions. This requires the manager to do a deep dive of learning into whether this creates more problems than it solves. New systems and processes take an enormous amount of time and effort to implement. Those who do it often, "exercise" their ability to do so, and again, it becomes easier.

What is going on in the rest of the company: There is an ENORMOUS opportunity in most companies for sharing of knowledge amongst department heads. There are so many needs that have already been solved by other departments that could simply be "plugged into" another department without reinventing the wheel. Also, if you satisfy that curiosity about how another department operates, it simply adds to your tool chest of knowledge when they start passing around promotions. Either way, more knowledge isn't going to be a bad thing at all.

Each time you run across something that you do not know, or do not understand, know that you have come across an opportunity. Those who seize the most opportunities usually win in the end. So don't avoid what you don't know, run towards it.

LESSON ASSIGNMENT: Go to a department that supports yours and learn how to do one task that they do to support you. Alternatively, go to a department that YOU support and learn how they do one of their tasks that you support. By going both upstream and downstream you will get the benefit of learning how your operation fits into the whole, this perspective can help lead some of your decisions.

The next step is to leverage this learning into the operations of your own department by sitting with your best agent for a day and observing how they work and what challenges they face.

Manage Your Fun at Work

Diary Entry #14 – May 15th

"I try to learn from the past, but I plan for the future by focusing exclusively on the present. That's where the fun is." ~*Donald Trump*

"Winners have simply formed the habit of doing things losers don't like to do." ~*Albert Gray*

· · · · ·

One of my topics in this book is doing what you "need to do" at work, not just what you'd like to do, or what is easy to do in the chapter "Find The Work You Need to Do". Now I'd like to talk about managing what you "like to do", after all, as managers we try to manage everything right?

Hopefully you enjoy where you work, what you do, and whom you work with, but inevitably there are a number of things you do not enjoy as much. So why is it important for you to manage your fun?

- *So you have the energy and passion to do what you don't like* – We are constantly pulled in a number of directions as managers, and we are constantly being watched as well. The quicker

98

and better we do tasks, the more we will be able to do. If you bring the same energy and passion to all of your activities you will see amazing results.

- *Getting through the tough days* – We'll all have those days and weeks that are just a bummer. Managing your fun helps you get through those times.
- *So you set the example for your staff* – Doing what is necessary is essential to being successful in your position. Doing it with "gusto" is essential to being able to move to the next level. Display this ability to your staff and you change the culture

That's great Cameron, so now how do you do it?

- *Find what you like to do* – Some of us like statistics and projects, some of us like talking to our staff, some of us like talking to customers. Whatever it is for you, identify it (and preferably them, i.e. plural).
- *Eliminate the binge/purge syndrome* – Find time in each day to do what you enjoy, and preferably space it out at intervals throughout the day. This will bring greater enjoyment to the day, and avoid the monotony of crunching through work you hate.
- *Create a reward for getting through a tough task* – The next time you are faced with a task you dislike, reward yourself for finishing it by placing a task you do like on the other side of it.
- *Look for what you enjoy IN what you don't* – If you can find that silver lining in the cloud of a crummy task and focus on that, it will have a big impact on what you bring to the overall task.

We aren't robots, and passion is like rocket fuel to performance, so try to find it in everything you do, or at least sprinkle it throughout your day. It will make your job easier AND more productive, a win-win in anyone's book!

LESSON ASSIGNMENT: Make a list of all of the tasks and things you like to do in your day to day work. Post that list next to your computer. The next time you are facing a lack of energy, or are trudging through a task you don't like, check the list and do something on it.

Don't Continue The Demoralizing Cycle

Diary Entry #15 – May 24th

"Enduring setbacks while maintaining the ability to show others the way to go forward is a true test of leadership." ~Nitin Nohria

"The ability to summon positive emotions during periods of intense stress lies at the heart of effective leadership." ~Jim Loehr

.   .   .   .   .

You must constantly be on guard to maintain your positive outlook. People are human, both employees and managers. What that means is that the larger your team, the more likely it is that you have all different kinds of people, with different tendencies and perspectives.

This was brought to my attention recently when a few employees came to me frustrated because I had not fattened the incentive pool more. Initially I was shocked, then I was frustrated, and then finally angry. I had spent an enormous amount of time getting the program approved by senior management, and it was in fact unique within the industry (most employees in our industry in similar companies received no incentive). Basically I felt that these employees were ungrateful.

I'd run into this before with my Supervisory staff, whom I had intentionally protected from long hours and stressful negativity, while the company was going through some difficulty (my methodology was that they were the face of management to the front line staff and therefore, to maintain a positive work environment, and thus positive productivity, I needed to ensure the Supervisors were fresh and positive). They had asked for more flexibility with shifts, a lighter workload, and generally griped about a bunch of very little things. Mind you, their peers within the organization were working longer hours, put in more negative situations, and had limited flexibility to do their work. Again, my hard work and thoughtful leadership fell on deaf ears, my staff was ungrateful.

The thought crossed my mind. "OK, why do I bust my butt doing right by all of my employees? I could just take it easy, do what most managers do, and they'll still be just as unhappy". What would have happened?

- Their unhappiness and dissatisfaction would have a demoralizing effect on me.
- I would stop caring about them, and their situation would get worse.
- They'd be even more unhappy and dissatisfied, bringing even more issues to me, further demoralizing me.
- I'd care less, they'd be more dissatisfied, etc, etc, etc.

Luckily, after stewing for a couple hours I realized what would happen if I gave into my passions, so I stopped. To mitigate these occurrences from happening in the future, I now try to remember the following:

1. If you deal with a large enough staff, you will always disappoint some with any action you take. It is human nature to want more, regardless of how good you have it. Do not

let this small minority (often less than 10% of your staff) dissuade you from doing your best for the majority.

2. It's important to (respectfully and tactfully) take credit for the good that you've done for you staff. So expose them to other businesses and departments, involve them in decision making where appropriate, and whatever else you can think of to help them remember all that is done for them.

3. Act slowly on any negative feedback. Whether it means taking a walk, or sleeping on it, you risk continuing the cycle if you react too fast.

So keep strong in your stance to do what is right for the business and for your staff, otherwise things could spiral right down the toilet.

LESSON ASSIGNMENT: Make a list of the Top 5 things you are proud of having done for your staff. The next time you are disappointed by some of the feedback you receive, come back to this list for a pick-me-up before you respond.

P.S. If you can't come up with five things, get to work on that first.

Re-Finding That Newbie Idealism

Diary Entry #16 – May 25th

"I rate enthusiasm even above professional skill." ~Edward Appleton

"Sometimes the best way to learn is to return to the fundamentals." ~John Maxwell

· · · · ·

After a couple decades in the business world, after a decade in the industry, and after a couple years in your position, it's easy to become a little more…how do I say….monotone in your thinking. Peers throw out ideas, and you've seen them before. The boss has a new initiative, but it's really just his clockwork quarterly "big idea". Your employee comes to you with a new process for improving production, but it's very far reaching. So you either go along with a "ho-hum" attitude, or shoot holes in everything.

But what if you threw your all into it? What if you reacted to everything as an opportunity? What if you treated it all as if it was your first day on the job, with all the hope and possibilities that entailed?

That very experience that leads you to believe you've seen it all before is what could push something you've seen fail so many times over the finish line finally. Keeping our passion at the forefront of our work is one of our most important leadership traits and shows your employees and peers the passion that leads to success. Your experience matched with youthful enthusiasm can be a very potent asset to the company.

So what do you do when you find yourself losing your passion? I say you have two options:

- *Start Big* – Do something you've never done before, or that you've never even seen done before in your industry. Preferably one where you control all of the strings (no approvals from outside your area of responsibility). This should help get those "new manager" juices flowing.
- *Start Small* – Pick a small project with a high probability of success. Again, preferably one where you control all of the strings. See it through to completion, then pick another small one and see that to completion. This builds new momentum success after success.

Of course, I suppose there is a medium option as well, but the important thing is to snap yourself out of the doldrums and re-excite the productive use of your experience. Remember what Thomas Edison said: "I have not failed. I've just found 10,000 ways that won't work."

The other thing to look at is who you are spending your time with. If you spend time with the grizzled veterans of the company, then you will begin to see things as they do. However, if you spend more of your time with the new employees, with the new managers, and with those who are accomplishing the most within the company. If you find yourself losing passion, maybe a change of scenery will help.

LESSON ASSIGNMENT: Get with your newest employee and ask them what project they would like to start that would have an impact on the operation. Then work the project through to success WITH them.

Focus on Big Things, Not Just What Can be Measured

Diary Entry #17 – May 26th

"The greatest enemy of knowledge is not ignorance, it is the illusion of knowledge." ~Stephen Hawking

"There are so many men who can figure costs, and so few who can measure values." ~Unknown

. . . . .

"You cannot manage what you cannot measure" is one of the great maxims of management. And it is absolutely correct. But oftentimes there are easily measured items that have little impact on the organization that become the focus of misguided or manipulative departmental managers. Sure we can measure it, sure we can manage it, and sure we can push forth improvement....but does it mean a darn thing to the organization!

How many times have you been in a meeting and a manager has touted their improvement in some metric of only modest importance. This is a detrimental political sleight of hand. Regardless of what sports teach us, not all wins are created equal.

Some things are more important than others, and the LAST thing you want to do is lose focus on the big things (regardless of whether they can be measured), and trade that for some sort of useless data point.

Customer satisfaction is a notoriously "fuzzy" thing to attempt to measure. Have you ever attempted to measure the smiles of your customers when they interact with your employees and products? Of course not, but we can all agree that this is one of the most important measures of success for a company.

Now if you can come up with a few easily measurable items that lead into customer satisfaction it becomes easier. But oftentimes the drivers of this are not nearly as cut and dried.

- Repeat Customers (can you pull a report on that)
- Referrals (do you have any incentive to be able to track)
- Survey (be careful with the construction of it, but they can be valuable)

These are just a few things that may reflect customer satisfaction, or they may not in your case. The key is to try to find something that you can report on to both give feedback to your staff and to track performance.

Intuitively, Google knows that keeping its engineers happy spurs productivity, creativity, and shareholder value. But honestly, there's no measure of it. Google's former CEO Eric Schmidt once said that keeping his employees focused on work instead of where they are going to eat (employee dining facility), their commute (provided transit stops), and even where they are going to do their laundry (on site laundry facility), created more hours in their work day, but the ROI goes much further beyond that. It makes them happy, and therefore more productive and likely to be retained, and therefore drives value for the company.

Attempting to measure it is fruitless, but Google apparently believes these perks are well worth it.

P.S. There must be some data there somewhere because a notorious Google mantra is "what does the data show?"

So you should always endeavor to measure what you want to manage, but if it's important enough, don't pass it up for some easily measured (and improved) metric. Take what you can get, find a measurement somewhere, then get to work on these important things.

LESSON ASSIGNMENT: Come up with a list of the top 5 most important things to your organization (profit margin, sales, customer satisfaction, etc). Now come up with the top 5 things that DRIVE each of those items. Now see if you can measure any of those 25 smaller things (and for those you can't, see if you can come up with a way to find 5 things that drive those).

How To Use Your Strengths

Diary Entry #21 – June 4th

"To succeed in life we must stay within our strength zone but move out of our comfort zone." ~John Maxwell

"Live in terms of your strong points. Magnify them. Let your weaknesses shrivel up and die from lack of nourishment." ~William Young Elliott

.　　.　　.　　.　　.

There are plenty of books that talk about this, and truthfully, I don't know that I've read any of them. But what we see a lot of in business is people trying new things, and that is wise, but we must move into new things from the position of what we already do well to give ourselves the greatest chance for success. There are two (what I consider) obvious uses of strength; to address your weaknesses and to expand your area of expertise. Here's how to do it:

First understand yourself

- Do you know what your strength is?
- Do you know what you do well?
- Do you know where you thrive?

Now:

- Do you know what your weakness is?
- Do you know what you don't do well?
- Do you know where you struggle?

Now, how can you use what you do well to address what you don't do well? Yes, you should take your weaknesses head on, but it is safer (and oftentimes more effective) to leverage your strengths to do it. This isn't exactly rocket science, but business isn't usually that complicated, it just takes some finesse.

One of the quickest and easiest ways to help yourself based on this knowledge is to swap strengths and weaknesses with a peer. If you are terrible with spreadsheets, and your peer is an expert, maybe they can take some of the spreadsheet load off your hands. In turn, if you are good at something they struggle with, you can help them in return. The net effect of this is that both of you now have extra time to work on something more impactful, or address one of your weaknesses (like taking an Excel class in this example).

So now that you are spending more time operating within your strengths, let's take a step further by seeing if we can expand our sphere of influence and impact on the company and department. The first place to tackle is their weaknesses (their strengths are almost always being staffed). First you need to understand the company/department:

- What is the company's/department's weakness?
- What does the company/department not do well?
- Where does the company/department struggle?

Now based on this new list, you can see where there are opportunities for you to use your strength to make an impact on the company's weakness? Do this enough times and you will see your sphere of influence expand as well as your standing with the company.

LESSON ASSIGNMENT: Ask both a peer and a subordinate what two of your strengths are. Then ask them what your two biggest weaknesses are. This is neutral information to double check your own thoughts, and from this you have your starting point to assess what weaknesses to address, and what department and company opportunities you can utilize them in.

Discard Preconceived Notions

Diary Entry #23 – June 6th

"If past history was all there was to the game, the richest people would be librarians." ~Warren Buffett

"It's amazing what ordinary people can do if they set out without preconceived notions." ~Ben Stein

. . . . .

How often do you like to prove someone wrong? For me, there is rarely something I enjoy more (we all have our vices, what can I say). So why should we treat ourselves any different? First impressions and preconceptions are a useful tool in quickly filtering data in our all too hectic lives, that's why they are so prevalent. But as with all good things, there can be too much of it, and in this case they too often become a crutch. Or even worse, become an excuse for inaction.

Try to change your habit of using preconceived notions too much, by occasionally getting into the habit of doing a "double take". For instance, what if you changed the below three notions:

- These sorts of projects have never worked out.
- That person has never been able to contribute anything worthwhile.
- That piece of equipment never does as well as the salesmen say.

Into this:

- Why haven't these projects worked out in the past? What can we do to stop that from occurring this time?
- What is that person's strength? How can I leverage it for the greater good?
- Why do they say it isn't working as planned? Can we change some of our processes to make it more productive (cost/benefit analysis of course).

As we move along our journey as Supervisors and Managers we gain tools and wisdom along the way. This means we are better equipped today to properly take care of what we couldn't in the past. This quick 30 seconds to rethink what our initial impression of a situation can reap big benefits for us and the organization.

Now while it is probably not efficient to do the "double take" with everything, you can at least try it out on a few things and see if anything comes out of it. I think there are opportunities out there that we are missing because we are not focusing on the issues surrounding our preconceptions. Too simplistic you say? I would argue that simplicity is what we are usually after in business. And heck, it doesn't cost you anything to try.

LESSON ASSIGNMENT: Some of our worst preconceptions surround people. In this case, take your three worst employees based on your "gut feeling", could be for attitude reasons, performance reasons, etc. Now do a "double take" by asking yourself what they are good at? Then put them exclusively in situations where they excel and observe. From my experience at least one of them with turn around.

When the S#it Hits The Fan

Diary Entry #27 – June 27th

"Successful leaders see the opportunities in every difficulty rather than the difficulty in every opportunity." ~Reed Markham

"Example is not the main thing in influencing others. It is the only thing." ~Albert Schweitzer

. . . . .

When the "stuff" hits the fan, that's when real leaders shine. That's when you're put on a pedestal for all to see. Now I don't mean one of those "manufactured" emergencies that only matter in your own head, or that are the result of your own mistakes. I mean a crisis for the organization as a whole. It is in those moments that your people look to you, not primarily for direction (that's secondary). They look to you for how THEY should react. If you panic, they panic. If you remain solution focused, they will be solution focused. Emergencies can be large or small:

- There was an unexpected system failure that caused all systems to fail (except the phones for your customers to call in to ask what happened).

- The first week of the Holiday Sales Season wasn't even close to budget, there are now four weeks to make it up or some staff may lose their jobs.
- The 1,000 balloons for the big Grand Opening just blew away 2 hours prior to opening.

If it's a true emergency, they will WANT you to show them the way out. It doesn't mean you have to be a robot. By all means, acknowledge the importance of what is going on, but when you start feeling the panic, frustration, disappointment, sadness or anger set in, you must stay focused on the issue and its solution so that your staff can mimic your "solution focus". Your employees will be feeling enough of the emotions for you, and DO NOT need anyone to feed them at this time. This is when you become everyone's rock. If you show strength and focus, your employees will find the same for themselves. The key steps:

- *What is the plan?* – The single most important step is figuring out what to do.
- *Who is involved in doing what?* – Give specific direction.
- *Monitor progress and adjust as necessary?* – Every plan can be made better along the way.
- *Figure out what you learned once it is over?* – How to prevent the emergency or creating standard procedures for dealing with it next time.

By "sucking it up" yourself, you'll lead your employees towards "sucking it up" themselves and help all of you get through the emergency successfully.

LESSON ASSIGNMENT: Since it is best to not practice in the real world, set up five disaster scenarios and create a quick and concise plan for dealing with them.

- *Possible examples:* Power outage, flood, theft, inventory delayed by dock-worker strike, medical emergency with employee, medical emergency with customer.

The key is to practice quickly coming up with the steps to a solution and being calm doing so. Once you come up with five and have practiced with them. Get with a peer and have them give you a couple of scenarios verbally and see if you can come up with a plan right on the spot. If you can't, go back to the drawing board above, rinse, and repeat.

Covey: Focus on Big Rocks

Diary Entry #19 – May 30th

"Tactics without strategy is the noise before defeat." ~Sun Tzu

"The main thing is to keep the main thing the main thing." ~Stephen Covey

. . . . .

Too often we get caught up in all of the little things and do not carve out the large chunks of time necessary to take care of the big things. How many of us have said at the end of our day "well I didn't accomplish any of the things I was planning on doing today"? Steven Covey covers this brilliantly in the 7 Habits of Effective People, and it is one of the most important lessons I have taken from the book. If there was one thing you could do today, this week, this month, this quarter that would greatly improve the value of your department to the organization, what would it be? Now ask yourself what minutiae are so important that they are keeping you from that?

In today's workplace there is not enough time for everything, so you have a choice, sacrifice the big thing that can really improve your business, or sacrifice a bunch of little things that may or may not be essential? I think many of us fall into the trap of weighing all work equally which helps us to satisfy the most people or interests, but at what cost to the overall health of the department or company?

In practice, there will need to be balance, because some little things that are neglected too long become big things (that report you send to the Executive Committee every week still needs to be done, sorry). But oftentimes your staff can handle things in your absence, unless you have forgotten that <u>they do when you're on vacation</u>.

In my world I had initiatives to grow revenue through training and pipeline visibility that sat there for months because I was too busy with the little things that were keeping the operation running smoothly, but weren't adding much value and probably could have got along without me. If you focus on these large things and add the small things around them, you'll accomplish a lot more for your company.

For those who haven't focused on this before the best way is to pick one thing that if you accomplished it today you could say, "I really contributed to the bottom line today". Once you master the ability to get these 30 minute to 4 hours projects through to completion (it is usually irresponsible/impossible to be out of the operation for longer than that during a day), then extend it to a weekly project, then a monthly project, then a quarterly project. The key is to make your work about moving the operation forward, not just maintaining the status quo.

LESSON ASSIGNMENT: The last paragraph of this article describes what to do with the "project rocks", but your first assignment will be regarding tasks, not projects. Pick the most important task on your list each morning, and ensure it gets done. Then tomorrow, pick the two most important items, then three....and stop there. If you get your three most important tasks done each day you are WAY ahead of everyone else and may lose focus on your commitment to yourself, and it will take commitment. This builds some momentum with the more simple "tasks", then you can move on to a project.

You Can't Win if You're Whining

Diary Entry #38 – August 12th

"Ninety-nine percent of failures come from people who have the habit of making excuses." ~George W. Carver

"Hold yourself responsible for a higher standard than anybody expects of you. Never excuse yourself." ~Henry Ward Beecher

.   .   .   .   .

Let's just say it, don't whine, nobody wants to hear it, babies whine! Does anyone like that whiny, sniveling, loser??? One of the biggest things that keep people from ascending the ladder of success is "whining". And this behavior is not limited to the rank and file hourly employees, it also is exuded at the Executive ranks (we've all had THAT boss before).

There is a natural tendency to whine for several reasons, and we almost all struggle with it at some point. So what are the reasons and how do we stop ourselves? Here are the two biggest reasons for whining:

Excuses – The most common form of whining is in response to excusing a failure. Comparisons, lack of resources, lack of training, acts of God, the alignment of the stars, etc, etc, etc. At some point you failed, and you try to come up with some excuse that is out of your control (and therefore eliminating any blame on you). Quite frankly, a great manager controls as many things as possible. If you are pleading with your superiors about all of the things that were out of your control, you are showing yourself in the worst possible light. Instead of whining, talk about the things you controlled, the things that went right, then discuss what occurred that went wrong, what you learned, AND what you will be doing about it. Excuses and whining are backward looking actions, you need to be looking forward.

Injustice/Unfairness – The most common way that this comes about is with double standards. We whine about how other managers or other departments get preferential treatment or aren't held to as high of a standard as others. The question I have: Why are you focusing on things outside of your area of responsibility instead of focusing on improving your own operation? And trust me, your superiors are asking the same question about why you aren't focused on yourself. Keep your focus on your own area, and let your superiors worry about the other operations.

One of the best ways to show maturity and wisdom in your current position is to eliminate whining and replace it with insight. It is one of those things you will need to vigilantly battle, but one that will serve you extraordinarily well if you are successful.

LESSON ASSIGNMENT: The next time you are inclined to whine, don't try to explain or offer an excuse….just shut your mouth. Do this the next five times you are tempted to whine (when you think about it, we whine to employees, peers, and bosses, so you have plenty of opportunities). Master the art of not whining, THEN work into more constructive responses where you explain what you saw, what you learned, and what you will be doing about it.

Consistency is the Key to Success

Diary Entry #44 – August 31ˢᵗ

"Success is more a function of consistent common sense than it is of genius."
~An Wang

"Continuous effort not strength or intelligence is the key to unlocking our potential." ~Winston Churchill

·   ·   ·   ·   ·

As the old adage goes, "Rome wasn't built in a day" and while we would all like overnight success and a rocket ship to the C-Suite, the reality is that the path of success is a long and arduous one and the true test is what we do over time.

Just like the stock market, there is a premium paid for consistent delivery. Your staff and your boss are looking for consistency. The true power of your actions comes from their consistent delivery, as you break through resistance and establish an environment of trust (nothing breeds distrust like constantly going back on your prior decisions, or letting them die on the vine from neglect). Unfortunately this is all too uncommon in the business environment of the day, but that will help you stand out from the managerial crowd.

- For your staff, it is the consistency of expectations, policy adherence, and most of all demeanor (how you deal with crisis, how you carry yourself, and support your staff), among other things.
- For your superiors, it is all about consistent results and consistent proactive dealing with issues as they come up.

Consistency dispels any thought that you are lucky, consistency proves your conviction, and consistency reaps the slow and steady reward for your work effort. A thousand small improvements add up.

You are rarely rewarded for your application of excellent management techniques in the short run, the true reward of respect comes over time. If you consistently stick to your guns (ensuring those guns are the correct ones) your star will rise with greater and greater speed as you build a reputation of excellence with both your staff and superiors.

LESSON ASSIGNMENT: Identify one thing that you should do consistently. Create a calendar, and mark off for every day you do that thing. After a month add another, then after another month, add another one, etc.

Get in Dialogue with the Market

Diary Entry #50 – September 25th

"Leadership and learning are indispensable to each other." ~John Fitzgerald Kennedy

"Anyone who stops learning is old, whether at twenty or eighty. Anyone who keeps learning stays young. The greatest thing in life is to keep your mind young." ~Henry Ford

.   .   .   .   .

While the best ideas generally come from your customers and employees, the second best often come from others in your industry. If you want to move ahead in your career, you need to tune in to some.

One thing that separates Supervisors and Managers from VPs and CEOs is what they see and what they are surrounded by. Supervisors and Managers by necessity must be focused on their operation, in all of its details. While VP's have a similar need to focus on their areas of responsibility, they also have YOU to assist with that. This leaves them with the time to look at trade publications, be on industry organizations, and generally be able to look beyond the present issues to the future. This helps them fulfill their role of being proactive. What they look at outside the company, also should be what you look at outside the company:

- *Industry magazine and trade publications* – Believe it or not, no matter how obscure or small your industry may be, there is almost always a magazine or trade publication that covers the current issues and trends. Try subscribing to one or two and you'll be surprised at what you find.
- *Industry websites* – The above mentioned publications also have websites, but there will also be more online only websites and blogs that cover your industry. A good way to find some of the more prolific is through your LinkedIn profile and the "LinkedIn Today" tab. This pulls articles based on your profile and is a great place to start.
- *Industry panels or organizations* – Not all of them are for VPs and CEOs only. Oftentimes they have more standard memberships available as well. Look to choose those that hold mixers and events that will allow you to network with peers. This is a great way to both build your network and share ideas.

Like all things, you are only going to get what you give, so whether it be spending some of your free time reading industry publications, or talking about some of the things that have worked for you at the next industry mixer. Be ready to expend at least a little more effort.

They say you need to dress for the job you want, not the job you have. Well the same goes for the subjects you talk about. So supercharge your career, find new solutions to your problems, impress your boss, impress your employees, and become a more well-rounded employee by tapping into these areas!

LESSON ASSIGNMENT: Subscribe to one industry magazine and one general business magazine. Read them from cover to cover. If a $12 subscription helps you get a promotion with a

$5,000 higher salary, that's probably a good investment right? You can start with the four general business magazines below:

- Fast Company
- Forbes
- Fortune
- BusinessWeek

Be Dissatisfied With Your Performance

Diary Entry for Book #4

"Don't measure yourself by what you have accomplished, but by what you should have accomplished with your ability." ~John Wooden

"Keep your head, heels, and standards high" ~Unknown Author

. . . . .

Recently I tackled the management of a new department. Quite frankly, the bar had been set very low for me as the department had been horrendously mismanaged prior, so getting more productivity out of the staff was relatively easy. As I set things in motion, and as the improvements began compounding on top of one another, and as the accolades rolled in, I kept tempering my achievement by saying "Yes, but it could have been faster….it could have been better…..wait till I refine the process for the second time". In short, even though everyone thought I was a rock star, I knew I could have done more.

It comes with a certain wisdom that you realize you can give your best, you can create fantastic results, yet you are wondering how you could have done it even better. Think about the track star who wins a gold medal, but tells the announcer that he could have been quicker out of the blocks, his form broke down

130

a few times, and that while he is thrilled to win, there are better times on the horizon (BUT HE WON A GOLD MEDAL!). It is the separation of achievement and potential.

Your potential as a manager is so much greater than your achievements thus far. It is an old saying that companies are most vulnerable when they are at the height of their success, so too are managers. The reason is that they start thinking of themselves as the teacher, not the student. And when learning stops, so does progress.

This does not mean that you are to be moping around because you know you're not perfect. What we are striving for is excellence, not perfection, and excellence is always a work in progress. I didn't come home after all of those accolades and all of that success depressed because I didn't achieve more, I was really happy with my performance, but I knew there were ways (not always little tweaks) that I could have elicited better results. I was comfortable with that, and so should you.

One word of caution be careful about being dissatisfied with other's performance. You must be very careful when critiquing other's performance to not come across as someone who is never satisfied and is a perfectionist. The key is to build a culture of excellence AND learning, and that even the company's greatest successes yielded lessons that could be used in future endeavors. Do that, and you are on the way up the career ladder.

LESSON ASSIGNMENT: Take the top three achievements in your professional life (include some personal achievements if you are starting your career) and write down all of the ways those achievements could have been made even better. Now ask yourself what lessons you learned that can be applied to the next achievement. And BANG! You're now learning from success.

Seize The Opportunity

Diary Entry for Book #5

"When opportunity comes, it's too late to prepare." ~John Wooden

"The secret of success in life is for a man to be ready for his opportunity when it comes." ~Benjamin Disraeli

. . . . .

Sometimes when you have a goal or task, it simply won't work in your current environment. You need to be patient and wait for the situation to change and/or the opportunity to present itself. Oftentimes you need to make several moves along the way to get there.

What am I talking about you ask? For the most part your highest priority items will always be front and center and you will be actively working on them, but what I am talking about here are the priority B items that are priority B items because:

- You would "like" to get them done, but don't necessarily "need" to get them done
- They don't have a pressing time component to getting done.
- There are political or budgetary concerns that play into their implementation.

Things like:

- Hiring for a brand new position.
- Re-dividing responsibilities between team members.
- Purchasing an extra forklift for the warehouse.
- Cleaning up the storeroom and supply room.
- Pitching a new process between departments.
- Switching around the desk layout in the department.

Whatever it is, it is just not in the cards in the current environment, or is a chronically de-prioritized item (seriously, when was the last time anyone cleaned or organized your supply room?). So how do you set yourself up to seize the moment and opportunity when it presents itself?

- *Make sure you are clear on what is needed* – Keep a list of things you need to work on, accomplish, etc. If you don't write it down and don't look at it every week, you won't be ready when the opportunity is there.
- *Identify the obstacles in your way* – What needs to change? What would the path look like to your goal?
  - Does your boss not see the need – wait till they do.
  - Is it budget related – wait until the return on investment is obvious. "This could have been prevented if we had _____"
- *Keep your eyes open to the situation* – Sometimes the solution comes from a different angle, don't be dogmatic.
- *Shape the world when you can to match that path* – Oftentimes we can make small decisions that make the end goal easier to get to.
- *Pounce before the opportunity disappears* – Self explanatory, you may only get one shot at the stars aligning.

Being able to seize the opportunity to do what you want to do for your business and department is key to moving things forward and showing progress to your superiors. It's also fun to knock out a few of these items off your to-do list that you weren't sure you were able to get into action.

LESSON ASSIGNMENT: Start writing down things that come up that fit into one or both of these two categories. A) Things that have been on the to-do list for your department for more than six months (constantly de-prioritized items, B) Things that cause issues/problems repeatedly, where you say "If we only had _____ we wouldn't keep running into this". The fact you haven't addressed the things in these two categories is indicative of "Priority B" status. Review this list weekly and keep an eye out for the "perfect time" to be able to address them

Projects:
When All Eyes Are Watching

Don't Let Timelines Slide

Diary Entry #10 – May 10th

"Time is the scarcest resource and unless it is managed nothing else can be managed." ~Peter Drucker

"It takes less time to do a thing right, than it does to explain why you did it wrong." ~Henry Longfellow

. . . . .

It's called crunch time. These moments happen in sports all the time, it's the moment when the game is on the line and it comes down to one play. In business, it's usually about the timeline itself: the end of the quarter, end of the year, or more common, a milestone in a project.

If you want to be a high performing manager, you will need to FIGHT to keep your timelines intact. Most operations see timelines slide constantly, so if you are able to maintain yours consistently it will make you stand out for sure. Honestly, timelines are usually such a joke in most organizations, that this one trait could put you in line for a promotion. But it isn't easy (otherwise everyone would do it) and it takes a lot of effort:

It takes communication – The first and most important step is to communicate the timeline AND what the timeline is for each of the individual tasks.

It takes work – This should go without saying, but it's going to take effort. You will probably need to pull a late night to maintain your timelines (and most likely at least a few). So be ready.

It takes focus – You need to be on top of people, you need to follow up on progress, and you need to ensure they understand what the project needs, RELENTLESSLY.

It takes foresight – You need to see your problems before they become problems. If you correctly see where your issues may lie, you can take steps to mitigate the risk by following up or setting up contingencies.

It takes flexibility – Regardless of how well you prepare, there will be some delays that are out of your control. Wherever possible, you must build in some extra time to account for these. It may not be possible in all instances, but it is absolutely necessary wherever you can.

It takes favors – You need to have built up enough goodwill to get that "little extra effort" from others (you can't do it yourself). So when crunch time hits, you aren't standing alone.

In my experience, you'll need all of these to consistently be able to meet timelines. Now if your upper management has set completely unreasonable timelines (not an uncommon practice) then this will at least help you keep closer to them than your peers. But that is a different topic for a different time.

Following through on what you say you will do is the hallmark of any great career. If you can manage time and your timelines you will gain the necessary trust from your superiors to move onward and upward.

LESSON ASSIGNMENT: Start a "timeline score sheet" for your performance. Every time you are given a deadline, write it down on the score sheet. See how long you can keep the "timeline met" streak alive.

A Kick Butt Roadmap to Success

Diary Entry #30 – July 3rd

"Quality is the best business plan" ~John Lasseter

"The results of quality work last longer than the shock of high prices."
~Author Unknown

. . . . .

The words of my CEO still ring in my ears, "first we make it good, then we make it cheaper, then we make better, and then we make it faster." That was the simple roadmap for my company. Year one was nearing completion, we had accomplished step one, and with the budget process for year two underway, we were about to lock in step two. He was reiterating the importance of steps one and two and was setting the stage for steps three and four. I couldn't believe I hadn't heard it before. Afterwards I shared the idea with some of my staff, and ended up explaining away much of their resistance:

1) <u>Make it Good</u>: If your product or service isn't good, nothing else matters, you won't need to worry about steps two through four. A quality product or service must be your first focus and priority.

140

2) <u>Make it Cheaper</u>: Once you have a quality product or service, you should focus on the cost of producing it. It is important to focus on your <u>current</u> procedures as they are what you know best. Once you have optimized your current cost structure, you can explore new methods, suppliers, distributors, etc. to get the most out of your sales. This step comes second so you can pay the R&D to make the product better in step three.

3) <u>Make it Better</u>: Competition can be a bear, so what worked yesterday isn't going to work today, and sure as heck isn't going to work tomorrow. Making your product better will lead to repeat customers (see Apple iPhone model) and will tap into customers whose needs weren't satisfied by your original. And always remember that if you aren't making your product better, your competitors probably are.

4) <u>Make it Faster</u>: Process improvement can lead to cost benefits (just-in-time shipping leading to lower inventories), improved service (speed to market and support), and even new products and services.

It seems somewhat simplistic, but the best things usually are. What we see in our world is that we are usually just focused on Step 1, then Step 2, and then just keep working on Step 2. Don't stop there, Steps 3 and 4 can make the product or service cheaper as well.

What is more, once you have gone through all of the Steps once, it is good to go back to Step 1 and make any scope adjustments to "Make it Good". The odds are that the consumer has changed since you first tackled this step and you will need to make some adjustments.

Once you've mastered the first round, you wash, rinse and repeat over and over and over again until you are on the top of your industry or on your way to that promotion! Magnificent!!!

LESSON ASSIGNMENT: What stage of the process is your department in? Find that out, then set up your plan for working on the next step, then repeat the cycle.

Using Relay Teams in Business to Win

Diary Entry #37 – August 9th

"Great acts are made up of small deeds." ~Lao Tzu

"Nothing is particularly hard if you divide it into small jobs." ~Henry Ford

•   •   •   •   •

We've all been there, we bust our tail getting the report finished and polished, but don't have the energy to take action on the data held within. We spend all week getting the new product ready to launch, but don't have the energy to actually sell or service it once the doors open. Think of it this way; it's like Christmas morning, where you are given a great new toy to play with, except you were the one who had to stay up all night assembling it, so you don't have any energy to play with it.

You use too much emotional capital getting it ready, but don't have enough left over to finish the job. This is one of the BEST reasons to delegate tasks. It takes a lot of trust and energy to delegate, but if you don't, you may not be able to actually get the full benefit of anything you create.

This is the hallmark of great project management. Think of the process from start to finish as a relay race and divide up the tasks, then celebrate the results as a TEAM. This may already be occurring in a number of areas, but for those tasks/projects your department controls from start to finish, this can be a HUGE benefit.

Our focus as Supervisors and Managers needs to be on using information to make informed decisions and actions. Our focus shouldn't be on preparation of that data. To do so takes time away from valuable tasks for the organization, and fills up our time with things that perhaps one of our staff members could handle.

Another area of this concept is to consider working with peers to accomplish the same thing on higher profile or more complex tasks or projects. This can have the added benefit of creating more collaboration.

Truthfully, this is one reason consultants often have the easiest job in the world. Your business provides them with the information, and they have the energy to use it in the best way for the business. To use a sports analogy, they are the fresh pair of legs you bring in as a substitute near the end of the game.

Be your own consultant by breaking tasks into pieces of a relay race.

LESSON ASSIGNMENT: Take one of your next tasks and break it up into its step by step components, then divide it up amongst your staff. What you add is a component of action at the end, which is your responsibility. In this way your focus is action, not preparation.

Passion Before Process

Diary Entry for Book #6

"One person with passion is better than forty people merely interested." ~E. M. Forster

"You get the best efforts from others not by lighting a fire beneath them, but by building a fire within." ~Bob Nelson

. . . . .

Looking for that Trump Card for success over your competitors? Looking for an absolute guaranteed way to get the best out of your staff? Like most things, it is simple yet extraordinarily difficult; it is Passion.

Passion is the way to motivate employees to do more than as little as possible.

Passion is the ultimate force multiplier. It brings about focus in the individual, yet is contagious to the team. Companies can be good without passion, maybe even great. But they will get absolutely CRUSHED by a competitor who is able to elicit passion from their staff. The same goes for departments as well.

145

Can you think of a department or boss who everyone wants to work with? Yep, you got it, that's the one eliciting more passion.

One of the things that Passion does is to create buy-in and follow-through in new and existing processes. Too often, we as managers and supervisors have an extraordinarily difficult time getting our staff to follow the processes we put into place. If we can't get our staff to follow the process (or plan), then we face the potential for the plan to be diverted into unforeseen and unintended consequences. This stalls the forward momentum of the department and company as we try to put band-aids on the problems or try to resuscitate the plan. In your worst case scenario, this becomes a permanent stalling of forward progress.

The solution – Focus as much on passion as the process

That may seem like a bold plan, maybe even reckless when considering the time needs of implementing a new process, but it is time well spent. A process has more of a chance to die out if there isn't passion to jump start it when it hits a few roadblocks (which we know will happen from time to time), or just when fatigue sets in. So what are some of the things to consider?

- *The best passion is tied to something BIG* – The processes with the biggest upside and/or biggest impact on the company both elicit the most passion and require the most passion.
- *The process needs to consider the people* – It is all too easy to treat your staff like robots. Always consider the "human element" and their wants/needs whenever you are creating a new process or plan.
- *Refresh the passion* – Come up with means to recharge the batteries throughout the process (milestone celebrations, achievement celebrations, etc).
- *Winning* – The simplest form of passion is the yearning for achievement. Personal achievement is the shortest-term of

these, but if that can be tied to team achievement, then to department achievement, then to company achievement ....well now you've got something.

So before you roll out your next project or next process improvement, be sure to spend time on addressing the human side of the equation. It's an insurance policy on a successful implementation.

LESSON ASSIGNMENT: Create a contest around one of your most common processes (reservation entry, register checkouts, phone calls, etc). Make it fun, make the prize fun, and make it public with daily updates. This gives you practice eliciting some personal passion to win in your staff. Next step, do a similar contest with teams. The final step, find a way to elicit passion when implementing a new process or procedure.

Embrace Change

Diary Entry for Book #7

"Kings fear change. Leaders crave it." ~Seth Godin

"Winners must learn to relish change with the same enthusiasm & energy that we have resisted it in the past." ~Tom Peters

"It is not the strongest of the species that survive, nor the most intelligent, but the one most responsive to change." ~Charles Darwin

.   .   .   .   .

Change isn't a whole lot of fun most of the time. It takes a lot of work, and you're never entirely sure if the outcome is going to meet your expectations. But change is not only a natural part of business, it's a natural part of life. The quicker you realize that you will be constantly "reinventing" the way your department/company does their business, the easier it will be. And if you get in the practice of constant improvement and change, you will see your success increase exponentially. A boss once told me "change is a muscle, and the more exercise you put in, the stronger it gets, and the better you perform".

This metaphor of a "change muscle" is important because one of the greatest inhibitors of change is fear. We fear we are going to waste our time, we fear that the outcome won't be what we want it to be, we fear the unknown. As we exercise our change muscle, we begin to realize that most of these things we fear regarding change aren't anything to be afraid of. Rarely is it a waste of time, rarely do we not learn something constructive from the effort, and the unknown doesn't house only bad things, often it houses unexpected great things.

So how do you get change right not only for yourself, but for your team? Below are a few principles and a few tricks to help you navigate change efficiently and effectively:

1. *Why?* – You must set in your own mind and in the mind of your staff why the particular change needs to take place. Is there a financial reason? Is there a performance reason? Is there a legal reason? The first barrier is understanding that the "Why" is worth the effort it takes to change. If your "Why" is compelling enough, change gets much easier.

2. *Build a team* – Now sometimes the change is small and it can be just you, but I recommend that you still get another pair of eyes on the change. For larger projects, perhaps bring on a few people. This builds more consensus and buy-in if it isn't just you and provides more resources for the rest of your staff when questions arise.

3. *Elicit feedback from the start* – You won't get it perfect at the start. The quicker you get the feedback, the quicker you can fix it and keep the momentum going. Feedback also builds buy-in as the person bringing it now has a stake in the effort. Recognize and reward feedback, and you will see your feedback multiply.

4. *Create short term wins or show the immediate improvement* – If you don't celebrate certain achievements along the way, it becomes more difficult for people to go along with

you, as they aren't reaping the benefit of their "extra" work.

5. *Make it last* – Once in place it's important to come up with a way of locking it in to the make-up of the department, otherwise it is too easy to slip into the old way of doing things.

6. *Look for the next change* – As I said, it is an ever-changing business climate, there's another change that needs to take place, best that you jump on it before it jumps on you.

These steps give you a great chance to manage whatever change is on the table. You won't always get it right, and not all changes will reap the rewards you want, but staying in the same place is actually the riskiest plan of all.

LESSON ASSIGNMENT: Work on your "Why" muscle as a means of building your change muscle. Start explaining why (succinctly please) when rolling out simple changes or initiatives. Start explaining why you are doing something the way that you are. The "Why" is probably the most important aspect of the change management process, so the more practice you get the better. After practicing the "Why" for two weeks, you can begin walking through the rest of the steps when you need to roll out a less than simple change.

Be Like Water

Diary Entry for Book #8

"Be clear about your goal but be flexible about the process of achieving it."
~ Brian Tracy

"Be like water making its way through cracks. Do not be assertive, but adjust to the object, and you shall find a way around or through it. If nothing within you stays rigid, outward things will disclose themselves."
~Bruce Lee

. . . . .

It is inevitable that you will encounter obstacles as you make your way through your career. The best of us find ways around those objects, we do not let them impede our progress. Too often we see people whose progress is stalled because they do not find a creative solution to an obstacle (whether a bureaucratic, personality driven, or otherwise), instead they choose to beat their head against the wall when there is a door right next to them. What we need to do is:

- *Know that obstacles are going to arise* – No project or operation is without difficulties, so accept the fact that you are going to run into some obstacles. Look for them so that you can be ready for them as soon as possible.

- *"Be like water" and be flexible in what the solution could be* – Can it be done simpler? How would you handle it if you ran the company? What things not in your possession could help?
- *Be prepared for the next obstacle* – There's probably going to be another one, so don't rest too much, be ever vigilant.

Now that last point brings up an interesting exercise, because as you overcome obstacles and challenges you gain wisdom along the way. It is best to put these into action right away. Things to consider when being flexible, like water.

- *What led to the obstacle* – Is it in your control? Is it something that can recur?
- *If you had it to do all over again, how would you approach it so that this obstacle never existed* – If you have an answer, then put it into place.
- *Does how you get around this obstacle effect other obstacles cropping up* – A good exercise to think about while you are getting around your current challenge so that you don't set off a string of issues.

One word of warning though: The ability to implement creative solutions is important, but please do not make the mistake of making solutions more complex than absolutely necessary. The key is to get around/through the issue as quickly and completely as possible, while keeping your eyes on the road ahead.

LESSON ASSIGNMENT: Begin asking yourself, "What is an out of the box solution to this problem" when you come upon a challenge/issue. Try to come up with something fairly impractical, but that would work if time, money, and politics weren't issues. This exercises your creative problem solving skills so that when you come across a problem that doesn't have a quick and easy solution you are ready to go.

Team:
You're A Player Not Just A Coach

Experimenting with Other People's Ideas

Diary Entry #7 – May 5th

"Take a method and try it. If it fails, admit it frankly, & try another. But by all means, try something." ~Franklin D. Roosevelt

"Never be afraid to try, remember, amateurs built the ark. Professionals built the Titanic." ~Dave Barry

. . . . .

I was reminded recently about trying out ideas that others think are great, but that you are skeptical of. A counterpart of mine and I were tasked with interviewing potential interns for the company and our boss was adamant about having a role-play component to the interview. I felt it was not reflective of the candidates ability as they would have little information on our product offerings, sales techniques, etc. which would result in them being even more nervous and not reflecting their capabilities.

What happened was that we were able to see who wanted the job most (they did their homework since they didn't have the information spoon fed to them), we got to see how they worked under pressure (role playing isn't typically fun for the candidate), and we were able to see how they did when they didn't have all of the answers (not an uncommon occurrence in business). So I was proven VERY wrong regarding my opinion.

There are a few traps we may fall into when trying out ideas we disagree with, and they must be dealt with:

- *Preparation* – Just like anything new, you need to look for where the risks are and mitigate them as much as possible. Remember: "luck favors the prepared". So do the prep work like you would if it was your idea.
- *Work it honestly* – You must give it your best effort from start to finish. It's easy to sabotage anything by half-assing it.
- *Evaluate it truthfully* – Ask yourself what you would be looking for if it was YOUR idea to take out any negative bias you may have.
- *Don't be dogmatic* – If it really isn't working, and I mean REALLY isn't working, then please don't waste time and resources.

So don't just rely on yourself and your ideas, give others their due. If you can experiment in a short and focused burst with minimal downside (if the role playing didn't really work, we could simply leave it out of our evaluation when determining which candidate we were interested in) then there is really little harm.

Often, as with your own ideas, you'd be surprised by what you learn even on failed experiments. The lessons you learn from preparing the idea, working the idea, and evaluating the results can be the springboard to discovering the next great idea to move the operation forward.

LESSON ASSIGNMENT: If your department is anything like mine, there are literally dozens of ideas that have come up to improve upon it. Pick one that is constructive (not ridiculous) that you have a difference of opinion about, and run with it. Remember, you must give it a fair shot, and look for things to learn along the way.

Interact with **People Better**

Diary Entry #11 – May 12th

"The most important thing in communication is hearing what isn't said."
~*Peter Drucker*

"As a leader, you're probably not doing a good job unless your employees can do a good impression of you when you're not around." ~Patrick Lencioni

.   .   .   .   .

Communication is one of the most important, if not THE most important, skill in almost any job. The great communicators tend to find their way to great leadership positions in the company. As we constantly seek to streamline everything in our work and personal life to increase our productivity, we end up stripping out the extras. "Just the facts" becomes the mantra of the modern world.

The problem with that doctrine is that we work in a "human" business environment in most cases, and those little extras that are left out, often have a cumulative effect. In no place do you see the negative side of that more than in communication:

- Face to face takes too long so we use the phone
- Phone calls take too long so we send e-mail

- E-mail takes too long so we send a text

Now compare the two extremes, the difference between a text message and a face to face conversation. Which method ensures you are understood? Which method is easier to convey your true intention?

All I have to do is ask you one thing: "Has anyone ever misread an e-mail of yours and thought you were intending something hostile?" Of course they have, it's the downside of all of the fantastic productivity we get from e-mail. Now let me ask you another question" "Would they have had that impression if you had called them?" The answer is most likely, of course not.

Now I am absolutely NOT saying that you should do away with texts, e-mails, or phone calls, but what I am saying is that there is room for a little balance.

- Every once in a while, when you feel like sending a text, send an e-mail
- Every once in a while, when you feel like sending an e-mail, call them on the phone
- Every once in a while, when you feel like making a phone call, run over and talk to them face to face

If you do these things you will establish greater rapport with the people you work with, AND be less likely to be misunderstood when something can be taken two different ways.

There's also a reciprocal benefit: If you increase the proportion of your communication that is conducted in the "higher engagement" communication styles you will find that you also receive more information in return. How they are doing, whether their project is behind, what they need from you, etc. Try it out, I know you'll be pleasantly surprised.

LESSON ASSIGNMENT: For one day, do not respond to a single e-mail with another e-mail. Either call the person, or go to their office to see them. For group e-mails, make an announcement, or pull together a quick meeting. Do this once a week for a month and watch your relationships with coworkers and staff improve.

How to Instill Ownership in Supporting Departments

Diary Entry #46 – September 7th

"No one who achieves success does so without acknowledging the help of others. The wise acknowledge this help with gratitude." ~Alfred North Whitehead

"I've been blessed to find people who are smarter than I am, and they help me to execute the vision I have." ~Russell Simmons

• • • • •

We talk a lot about ownership with our own staff, but shouldn't it also flow to other departments? Especially those who support us? In my experience, I.T. and Marketing in particular are two departments where the staff tends to go through the motions a bit. So how do you excite the people on those teams who work on your projects and support you to excel?

One way is to take their contribution to the next level. Usually these departments talk about project completion, but try framing the RESULT of project completion:

- "You rolled out a new Customer Account system which has led to new marketing efforts that increased revenue by $5,000,000 last quarter"
- "The new phone switch installation will decrease our maintenance costs by $200,000 over the next three years"

This puts their contribution in terms everyone understands (dollars), and also maximizes the perception of their contribution.

Another great way is to identify who YOU want to work on your next project, and preferably someone who doesn't get the recognition they deserve:

- *Find the person* - I use the example all of the time of the "one" person that everyone calls in IT because he/she actually has the answers, it is this sort of person whom you want to reach out to. Similar to that is the person who you reach out to because while they may not know the answer, they have the professionalism and initiative to find the answer for you.
- *Bring them in* - Ask about making them your point of contact. Either request they head up your next project, or at least ask the project/account manager to utilize them as "grunt" labor (doing the tasks that the project/account manager doesn't want to). Once you find who you want, just find ANY way to get them into your operation and project to assist.
- *Spotlight* - Give them a taste of the spotlight by making a point to have them give an update on some portion of the project in a meeting or conference call. This instills ownership and lets them know that they are going to get credit for their work (too often this may not be the case in their native department).
- *Support* – They may be new to this sort of thing, so you need to be prepared to hold their hand a little more. Be sure to review their work, give feedback, and let them know that you wanted them on this project.

- *Quickly Give Credit* – You may have needed to call in a favor from the other department head, so ensure that you give credit to their boss, their bosses boss, and of course the employee themselves. As the old management maxim goes: "reward what you want to see more of". You'll get the best out of other departments when you give back to them.

Try to frame the contributions of others in a more powerful way in the future. Also look to reach out and identify the best in other departments, and you may find that your department is the one that truly benefits from their assistance.

LESSON ASSIGNMENT: Identify two rock stars in other departments that either support your current operation, or will be assisting on a project. Then reach out to their respective bosses and ask for them to be assigned to the next initiative for your department. Then follow the steps above.

Get People on Your Side

Diary Entry #31 – July 4ᵗʰ

"We build too many walls and not enough bridges." ~Sir Isaac Newton

"Leadership has a harder job to do than just choose sides. It must bring sides together." ~Jesse Jackson

. . . . . .

I credit a large part of my career success to being able to establish trust with peers. Being a trusted member of a team is essential to your career development, as the most important network you can possibly establish is the one inside your own company. These networks have led me to new positions, promotions, assignments on high-profile initiatives, assistance when most needed, and most recently, job security ("don't get rid of him, he's fantastic"). If you don't have the respect and assistance of your peers, you undoubtedly will find your job much more difficult. Do you want to know how I do that most effectively?

I respect and encourage their insight – People have different experiences and skills, and I insist that everyone has something I can learn from (yes, I mean everyone). By asking for their thoughts on matters, or participation in projects, I not only play to their vanity (though that seems a little more devious than it is intended to be), I also have an opportunity to learn from them. People want to be included, and if you are the one including them, they will be appreciative.

I make myself available for them – Rarely am I "too busy" to assist someone when they call upon me. 15 minutes isn't going to throw my whole day off, and if they are asking for more, they are usually going to be flexible in how you give your time and expertise. It makes me a resource for them, again something that they appreciate, and it also opens the doors to asking them to assist me. One favor begs the next. It also shows that I respect them since I am willing to always make time for them (you do the same for the VP don't you).

I praise them for their insight and accomplishments publicly – The greatest thing you can possibly do in business is praise others publicly, especially in front of their boss. Nothing will endear you to others quicker. Try it and you will quickly agree with me.

Now many of you will simply call this basic manners, but we sadly find few of those in most businesses. If you do the above three things consistently, you WILL stand out from the crowd. As managers we are often too busy attempting to show why we are better than our peers, rather than being the orchestrator of synergies between everyone. Also, you will find yourself in a better environment (friends are always a good thing) and more productive (as you increase the level of teamwork in the organization).

LESSON ASSIGNMENT: Probably the most powerful of the above techniques is the public praise technique, so let's tackle that first. During your next meeting, at the end, simply say "I'd just like to comment that Bill did a fantastic job with

_____ ". The blank can be exceeding his numbers for the month, helping you out with something, bringing a project in on time, almost anything. Don't rush it, wait until someone has really done something well, but if you are looking for it, it shouldn't take too long, maybe a week or two at most.

Don't "Save the Day", Be There From the Start

Diary Entry #34 – August 5th

"If everyone is moving forward together, then success takes care of itself."
~Henry Ford

"If you want to go fast, go alone. If you want to go far, you need a team."
~John Wooden

. . . . .

Listen, we all like to be the person that gets called upon to "Save the Day" for some sort of project/process, but I look at this as a failing unless you are brought into an entirely different department/division. Those who come in to "Save the Day" have shown up too late to the party, and in many cases the company has already suffered too much. What would have happened if they had been a part of the process to begin with? Would it have gone more smoothly? What negative impact on the company has occurred?

This has been brought to my attention many times in more "political" companies I have worked for. In these companies I have seen members of management wait in the wings while they hold their assistance/wisdom to the side waiting for the most politically advantageous moment to offer aid. To battle this phenomenon in your own life, I'd recommend:

- **Focus** – Whether aid is being offered or requested, the aiding party is most likely too busy to get involved deeply. Keep the aid limited to as short and focused a time as possible: A one-hour consulting meeting, one full day away from their operation, a once a day 5 minute phone call. This gives maximum bang for buck, and we all know we have other things that require our attention.
- **Come to aid graciously and non-threateningly** – Ensure the party knows that you are there to help the company and that they are the one in charge. Basically you are there to serve under their leadership. Then give them a positive review in front of some others. If you don't ensure that you are not a threat or glory-hog, then none of your contributions will be accepted by them anyway.
- **Don't shoot those who offer aid** – If you are the one being offered assistance, accept it graciously, but use the above two ideas in reverse. Respect their need to run their own operation and limit involvement to "bang for buck" moments. This also limits their potential "political" motives.

Synergy can be the benefit of scale, IF you do not engage in political wrangling and focus on using everyone's talents for the greater good of the company. Seek out advice from experts in the company, and offer your own wisdom graciously. <u>The companies that are best at this will be the ones who win!</u>

LESSON ASSIGNMENT: The next time you see a potential problem with someone's plan of action. SAY SOMETHING CONSTRUCTIVE. Don't criticize, don't step on their toes, don't try to take credit, just offer some constructive advice that they can make their own.

Don't Reinvent The Wheel

Diary Entry #39 – August 14th

"Good artists copy, great artists steal." ~Pablo Picasso

"Imitation is at least 50 percent of the creative process." ~Jamie Buckingham

· · · · ·

If you are a part of a larger corporation, you have a wealth of tools at your disposal that you may not be aware of: The work of others! A healthy company shares its knowledge freely across silos for the benefit of all. There is a more than likely chance that whatever you are struggling with, a peer of yours in another division/department has tackled it (or at least tried) before.

"Well Cameron, I don't work in a healthy company". And that is fine too, because the corporation does not define ALL of the managers of it. If you are open and collaborative, you can still leverage this. I've worked in several dysfunctional companies and have still been able to use the experience, reports, SOPs, and tips of others. To put it bluntly, you and your peers can rise above it. Here is the advice I have:

- *Offer to share first:* Odds are you'll hear about something in a meeting or e-mail chain. As the saying goes "be the change you want to see in the world". Open the door to collaboration by sharing FIRST and helping someone else out with a problem you have heard about.
- *Make it painless:* If you are asking for assistance, make it as easy as possible. Their time frame and your resources. These two things will break down much of the resistance.
- *Always offer to reciprocate:* Offer your resources in return, whether they be personnel, know how, etc.
- *Offer to give them credit (then do it):* Quickly and publicly let their superiors and peers know of their assistance to your efforts and the impact it had not just on your area, but on the company as a whole.

Follow the guidelines above and you'll be able to leverage the experience of others so you have more time to work on newer and more innovative ways to expand your business (and share with others). What do you have to lose?

LESSON ASSIGNMENT: Look at the improvements of your peers and see which can be emulated. But before you suggest it, make sure to pull the person, and your boss, together to go over it first. This way you can "suggest" and get the ball rolling, and your peer knows that they are getting credit for their assistance.

The Customer:
The Reason You Have A Job

Be a Customer Advocate

Diary Entry #24 – June 25th

"The absolute fundamental aim is to make money out of satisfying customers." ~John Egan

"There is only one boss. The customer. And he can fire everybody in the company from the chairman on down, simply by spending his money somewhere else." ~Sam Walton

.   .   .   .   .

Too many times we find ourselves in meetings where the arguments, strategies, and ideas are all one sided toward the benefit of the company. Of course this is important, but it must be balanced against the needs of the customer. As Stephen Covey says, look for the "Win-Win" in any situation.

I say be a customer advocate, because most people in the room will be the company advocate. Focusing on the company is what is easy to think of, but quite frankly, it is selfish and too often, short sighted. By being a customer advocate, by putting yourself in their shoes, you stretch your mind, you force yourself to look at processes the way your customer does. It is THIS behavior that creates impactful initiatives that improve the company's bottom line. Without a customer benefit, the company rarely receives a long term benefit.

The easiest way to do this is to set up a means to hear what your customers are saying. This is traditionally done through surveys, but typically these do not lead to obvious "actionable initiatives", and are instead, more of a temperature check on your current performance. I recommend creating an open channel of feedback with your line level employees. When they come off the sales floor, or production floor, ask them: "What struggles they had, or what struggles the customer had?" This can be anonymous, this can be written on their nightly drop, or this can be verbally communicated to the shift supervisor. The important thing is that you have 1-3 Positives and Negatives about the customer and the customer experience from each employee on each shift, whether it be stories or observations.

As always you must be consistent, and must show immediate action. But if you do this you will get a much better feel for what your customers are seeing, AND how it is going to make them feel. That way the next time you have a meeting, you can speak definitively on what impact something may have on your customer, or operation. And hopefully it will be heard.

Once you have received the feedback and begun to take action on it, you will naturally begin to gain a better understanding of your customer and be able to start making PROACTIVE decisions on behalf of the customer.

If you find resistance within your organization to this "new" way of thinking about decision making, do not feel alone as many companies struggle with this concept. The easiest way to break down barriers is to spell it out for the naysayers using simple "If-Then" logic. Always tying the "If" to the action and the "Then" to the result the company wants:

- "If we install this piece of equipment, then we will be able to ship merchandise to the customer faster. Then we'll both make the customer happier and save money on expedited shipping costs."

Remember, you are in business to service customers, serve them well and you will succeed.

LESSON ASSIGNMENT: Hang up a sign that says "What is best for the customer" in your department. Let everyone know that the guiding principle of the department is to constantly ask that question. If that is a little too much for you, then at least ask the question in the next meeting you have where you are discussing a product or process. Staying focused on what is best for the customer is what great Supervisors, Managers, and Businesses do to stay ahead.

The EASIEST Way to Fix Customer Problems

Diary Entry #29 – July 2nd

The golden rule for every business man is this: "Put yourself in your customer's place." ~Orison Swett Marden

"Treat others the way THEY want to be treated." ~The Platinum Rule

. . . . .

Dealing with customer problems effectively is one of the keys to any long running successful business. The cost of acquiring a customer is high enough that you generally don't want to lose them (though that is not always the case). But to what extent should you go to solve the problem? Do you put a Band-Aid on the issue? Do you use the "nuclear option" of a full refund or replacement? And how do you instill the correct attitude in your people? Simple:

Think of the customer's problem as your own

This concept conveys a wonderful amount of empathy (understanding and sympathy). But what every person also wants is their problem solved, so it is focused on being constructive as well. This is an easy to convey concept to your employees, but reaps big rewards from customers who might otherwise leave disgruntled.

Like many great ideas, it is simple, but can be tough to put into practice. Not all customers ..... how should I say this ..... encourage an employee to want to sympathize and assist them. That is why it's essential to give the "why" customer retention is important to your employees (for everyone's paycheck is a very reasonable explanation). Also, it is something that takes practice for most employees.

- Do they understand the issue the customer is facing?
- Do they understand why it is so important to the customer?
- Do they understand the option that best addresses the customer's need (and doesn't break the company's budget)?

I recommend spot checks with your employees. Just walk up and roll play the latest issue you dealt with or heard about. Do they meet the above three criteria? If you do this regularly your employees will be pros at keeping the company's greatest assets, its customers.

LESSON ASSIGNMENT: Take the next customer issue that is escalated to you and apply the "Think of the customer's problem as your own" principle. Document what you did and how you did it, and use that as an example with your team in tomorrow's pre-shift, team meeting, etc. Then do it with the next issue, and distribute the example in a similar format. Do this a total of three times, then solicit examples from your staff. The issue of customer recovery is important enough to be a daily topic.

Embrace Whatever Customer You Have

Diary Entry for Book #9

"Things turn out best for the people who make the best of the way things turn out." ~John Wooden

"Just because something doesn't do what you planned it to do doesn't mean it's useless." ~Thomas A. Edison

.　.　.　.　.

Sometimes we seem to be in a battle with our customers. Imagine:

- A day-care worker complaining about kids.
- A vendor at a stadium complaining about the loud fans.
- A bar owner complaining about drunks.
- A nightclub owner complaining that all he has in his place is a bunch of punk kids.

Sounds ridiculous, doesn't it? But I'd be willing to wager that someone that stares at you when you look in the mirror in the morning has done it once or twice.

The fact is that all of our customers are not in the perfect demographic that our business owners were shooting for (or maybe they are), but they are OUR customers and they are something to be cherished. Obviously, if it wasn't for them, there would be no need for us.

As a Supervisor or Manager, your task is to set the tone for how to deal with customers, the pleasant ones, the tough ones, and the strange ones. Are you going to go along with your exasperated staff, adding fuel to their fire by validating their feelings? Or are you going to attempt a paradigm shift and consider it a normal part of the day, like opening e-mail and stocking shelves?

Some phrases that help with this could be:

- "They are the reason we are here. If they were all easy, there wouldn't be much use for us"
- "Those customers pay my bills just as much as the others"
- "I'd rather they were here with us than over at (insert your greatest competitor's name here)"

But beyond the simple economic benefit, there are also opportunities to be had:

- Your most demanding customers, like a demanding coach, often push you to new heights of performance.
- Unanticipated customer demographics can discover unanticipated uses for your product and show you the way into unanticipated markets.

Find ways to serve them, embrace them, and see them as an opportunity to build your business. Don't be at war with them. Businesses evolve, evolve with them and you will see your success last longer.

Thank your lucky stars for every customer you have.

LESSON ASSIGNMENT: The next time you are faced with a difficult customer, a difficult customer issue, or a customer demographic that seems off, try to model the way for your staff and embrace them. As the old saying goes "If we don't take care of the customer, someone else will."

APPENDIX I

Management Compare & Contrast

Luke Skywalker vs. Darth Vader:

Often it's a good idea to take a look at two opposing sides and find out what makes them tick, what they do well, and what are their failings so that we can learn management techniques that can lead to success. So let's learn from one of the most famous father/son duos: Luke Skywalker and his father Anakin Skywalker (Darth Vader).

Beginnings & Education:

Both Luke and Anakin started out their careers in the corporate mailroom of the Galactic Empire, Tatooine. Neither was raised in an upper class family of privilege, they honed their skills outside the traditional schooling system. It was here that their desire for advancement blossomed, both dreaming of a corporate life of significance within the Galactic Empire. However, they found themselves with few options for advancement until they were "discovered" by their first mentors Qui-Gon Jinn and Obi-Wan Kenobi:

Similarity #1 – Neither Luke nor Anakin had the "perfect" background, family or education to be a success. But they DID have a desire for success, and SEIZED their opportunity when it arrived.

On The Job Training:

Both started their "schooling" much later than their Jedi peers. This created tension and distrust amongst their teachers and amongst their peers. Their reaction to this provides the first difference:

Difference #1 – Anakin was constantly trying to prove himself to his instructors and the Jedi Council in a constant grasping for respect (becoming a Jedi Master). Luke was more concerned about the end result and supporting that as best he could without personal ambition.

We see impatience in both Anakin and Luke, and in both cases, when they find out (through visions) that the ones they love are in danger (Anakin's mother, Luke's friends Han and Leia) they desert their assigned place (Anakin on Naboo, Luke on Dagobah) to rescue their loved ones.

Anakin responds out of vengeance (slaughtering the entire tribe that kidnapped and killed his mother) while Luke resists the temptation to give in to vengeance. That is an important moment in the movies, because it begins the real divergence in the lives of the two Jedi.

The apprentices both showed aptitude for piloting that they used under their mentors tutelage to launch their careers out of the mailroom and into the more impactful areas of the corporation. Both threw off the standard practices that were thrust upon them and charted their own more impetuous and reckless course through their tasks within the corporation.

But in both cases they relied on the instruction and assistance from their mentors, they did not act alone. This provided guardrails and allowed the broad strokes of their actions to fit within the overall Mission Statement of the company.

Lesson: PLAY TO YOUR STRENGTHS when starting while under a Mentor's tutelage. In this case Both Anakin and Luke used piloting to launch their career advancement.

Both lose their original mentors in a battle with a Sith lord (Darth Maul and Darth Vader) at a crucial time in the early stages of their development.

Similarity #2 – Both Luke nor Anakin recognized the importance of mentors. They each had their original mentors "leave the corporation" very early in their careers, but recognized they needed more training and quickly found replacements to help guide them in their career.

Working up the Career Ladder:

Their schooling was heightened by their timing. Anakin was tested thoroughly by the ongoing Clone Wars, whereas Luke threw himself into the Rebellion and thus gained practical experience. Both were obstinate with their Masters, never losing that feeling that they can do more, it may have been reckless, but showed confidence.

Similarity #3 – Anakin and Luke learned quickly that the best way to advance within the corporation was to make a tangible contribution. Neither was afraid to "get their hands dirty" and take action personally to get the job done.

Anakin had the benefit of the structure of the Jedi Council and the Republic to provide the means for recognition of his abilities and advance him forward within the corporation. Luke on the other hand did not have the advantage of recognition for his Jedi abilities within the Rebellion, he therefore moved much slower up the leadership ranks.

Difference #2 — Anakin's vanity began to show with the relatively constant awe and praise he received from his peers and superiors who recognized his extraordinary natural gifts. Luke on the other hand had his gifts relatively disregarded by his peers and superiors, and often mocked by Han Solo. This squashed the building of any pride which would prove important later on.

Into the C-Suite:

As Luke and Anakin moved into more advanced areas of leadership within the corporation that was the Galactic Empire, their similarities begin to fall away as traits like project management, corporate strategy, and structure and discipline come into play.

We do not get a chance to see Luke exhibit the traits of a great Project Manager on a large scale project (constructing his own Light Saber isn't what we are really looking for), but it is plain to see that Darth Vader is exceptional in this role. His oversight and personal involvement in the successful completion of the largest project in company history (the Death Star) proves this without a doubt.

He set this up through structure and discipline. There were timetables to be followed, and when they were not met, he personally saw to it that the schedule was put back on track. Those who were responsible for the delay were given one opportunity to correct their mistake, but if left uncorrected, had their employment terminated (which Darth Vader took care of personally without delegation).

Luke's approach to management of teams/projects is a more inclusive one where mistakes are expected and corrected, as he does with R2-D2 and C-3PO on several occasions. But he recognizes the benefits of having them on the team, and is flexible in his use of them. Darth Vader would have never allowed C-3PO to be a part of the mission to Endor (as the terrain was not suitable to his mobility), but by Luke including him, he was able to rescue the mission when it appeared to have reached a point of failure.

Difference #3 – Darth Vader is a strict disciplinarian and holds his staff accountable for achieving the objectives of the corporation without ANY exception. Luke is far more accepting of differences and mistakes and remains more flexible in his approach as the project evolves.

Darth Vader displays a knack for strategy very early on in his career that Luke simply does not display. All the way back in the mail room of Tatooine, Anikin comes up with the plan to secure the funding for repairs to their spaceship. Later in his career he develops the ability to mitigate more risk and be proactive with strategy to create a landscape where success is assured as he set traps with Lando Calrissian in the Empire Strikes Back, and in Return of the Jedi with the 2nd Death Star (feigning that it was not operational). Luke displays very reactive tendencies and poor strategic planning (what exactly was the plan when he went to rescue Han and Leia from Jabba the Hut??? How was that supposed to turn out successful???)

Where Luke excelled was in forming win-win alliances with people and with strategic allies as he did throughout the movies and especially with the Ewoks on Endor. Darth Vader's approach was more of a forced compliance role where the benefits were completely one sided towards him.

Summary

Luke Skywalker

Strengths:

- Selfless
- Mentorship
- Leads by example
- Creating a positive workplace

Weaknesses:

- Corporate Strategy

Anakin Skywalker (Darth Vader)

Strengths:

- Decisive action
- Project Management
- Corporate Strategy
- Corporate Structure and Administration

Weaknesses:

- Self absorbed
- Alliances
- Leads through fear

The safe bet for managing your Fortune 500 Company would, sadly, be Darth Vader. While he would not set up a positive workplace environment, he has demonstrated abilities of handling vast operations that Luke Skywalker simply cannot compete with.

If we are talking about a smaller business or even a medium sized business, I believe Luke becomes a more viable option as his skills come more to the forefront and his weaknesses do not come into as much play.

APPENDIX II

FIVE GREAT DEBATES

To Sandwich Criticism or Not

"Sandwich every bit of criticism between two thick layers of praise." ~Mary Kay Ash

"For a manager to be perceived as a positive manager, they need a four to one positive to negative contact ratio." ~Ken Blanchard

"Though bitter, good medicine cures illness. Though it may hurt, loyal criticism will have beneficial effects." ~Sima Qian

. . . . .

The Mary Kay quote above sparked one of the most heated debates I've ever had on my Twitter Page regarding whether to sandwich negative feedback between positive feedback (or at least end with positive feedback) or whether you need to cut to the chase and not water down your negative feedback. As with all of our decisions as managers, the question is what will result in the best outcome for the employee and the department? So what are some of the situations when you might use both techniques?

Sandwich Technique

- *When you want to maintain a positive workplace* – Always something we want to foster as managers. Too often, employees are given ONLY negative feedback. It is easy to see what is wrong, and that is often the focus of upper management, so it becomes your focus. The sandwich technique requires an overweighted balance of positive so as to support a positive work environment.
- *Deal with defensive employees* - Nobody likes criticism, so if you double the amount of positive feedback, you make the negative feedback easier for the employee to be open to accept and take steps to fix. It is too easy for employees to "shut the door" on you when you tackle negative feedback directly.
- *You are more concerned with long term wins and are risk averse* – The sandwich technique tends to get results over a longer period of time, which is not necessarily as good as getting results quicker. But this seemingly negative consequence is balanced against the fact that the sandwich technique is lower risk than direct feedback when it comes to an overall positive workplace environment.
- *Sensitive employees* – Some employees will shut down if you give them nothing but negative feedback. To fight that and to get your point across, the sandwich method is generally better.

Direct Technique

- *You've had a prior discussion* – If the issue continues to come up, you need to get firmer with the employee. Oftentimes discipline or termination loom on the horizon, so there needs to be a sense of urgency.
- *Serious issue* – If it is having a profoundly negative impact on the company's bottom line, or is a safety concern then there is no need to mince words. Using the sandwich technique waters down the seriousness.

- *Stubborn employee* – If the employee is very set in their ways or generally not open to ANY feedback negative or positive, you can't be soft in your approach. Direct feedback asserts your authority.
- *Need short term improvement* – If the situation needs to be remedied immediately, and you don't mind potentially having a cause/effect situation with something else, you can get improvement in that specific area better with direct feedback.
- *Smaller issue* – if it is a smaller issue, it just isn't worth making a production of the feedback session. Just jump right in.

As you can see, there is a general pattern to the situations that favor each technique and they beg three questions:

- *Culture of the department* – Is there a negative or positive vibe in the department
- *The employee* – Are they open to criticism? Which technique is going to get through to them?
- *The issue at hand* – Serious violation of Policy or a minor infraction? Repeat offense or first time with issue?

Based on your answer to these questions, you have your answer on which technique to use.

The Verdict:

To cut to the chase, you need to tailor it to the message and the person. There is no one rule for everyone and every situation. If you have to rely on how your feedback is received, whether in a sandwich or direct, for your employees to know how they are doing, then you have much bigger problems. The more frequent your feedback, positive and negative, the better it will be received and acted upon.

Personally, I believe the ideal situation is for you to have a positive working environment that allows you to give direct negative feedback in a timely fashion to your employees. It isn't a sandwich, it is a bowl of soup, where little pieces of negative feedback swim in a broth of positive feedback. Perhaps that is the real verdict.

Can You Change a Department or Company Culture?

"It's better to hang out with people better than you. Pick people whose behavior is better than yours and you'll drift in that direction." ~Unknown

"Company cultures are like country cultures. Never try to change one. Try, instead, to work with what you've got." ~Peter Drucker

"Be careful the environment you choose for it will shape you; be careful the friends you choose for you will become like them." ~W. Clement Stone

. . . . .

Changing a company's culture is one of the most difficult and challenging things in business, honestly, it is probably THE most difficult project to take on.

On the surface changing your company's culture is no different from changing how your company performs. Your focus shifts from prior performance norms to new norms along the lines of:

- *Purpose:* Why you are in business?

- *Deliverables:* What you need to provide to make your purpose happen?
- *Culture:* Values that align with your purpose?

What you are doing is changing what you pay attention to, and focus on. The difficulty comes from scale. If you have five employees you oversee, this can be accomplished relatively easy. If you have fifty, it becomes much more difficult. And by the time you get to three figures and above, well, that's an arduous job.

One of the reasons that scale is such an influencing factor is that people are naturally resistant to change, and if they can get away with doing it the "old way" a fair portion of them will, IF someone isn't there to hold them accountable and drive the change forward. For that reason, I propose the following path to culture change: Silos.

I've written before about the importance of sharing your exceptional performance with your peers and their departments, but sometimes to get there, you need to silo yourself. There isn't always a need to do so, but oftentimes those open lines of communication between departments can feed change resistance, negativity, and bad habits to your staff. The benefits of focusing on your own house first are:

- It's quicker to work with what you have
- You can take more ownership
- You increase your opportunities for success

However, it is important that you are subtle in your efforts. After all, you'll want to re-open the silo doors once you're rolling and have created some demonstrable "wins". So how do you do it:

- *Focus on "why the new way is better" not "why the old way was bad"* – Your staff, for better or worse, is attached to the way things function at present. Regardless of how much of a personal stake they took in the way things ran in the department, it is best to focus on the "new way being better" and driving that message home.

- *Focus on metrics controlled exclusively by you* – One of the greatest mis-steps that occur is focusing on things not entirely in your control. Your staff will grow defensive if the performance shortfall could be interpreted as someone else's fault.

- *Build teams within your department* – As you may be on a different path than your sister departments, this replaces the camaraderie experienced by the much larger "whole" of the company. It also allows you to evaluate and inspire performance amongst high and low performers.

- *Fill time and focus with internal tasks* – Whether it is a daily department pre-shift meeting, re-envisioning the layout of the office and duties, mentor training, or others. If you are not controlling where the staff's time is being spent, then they may seek to spend time and focus on areas you would prefer they didn't.

To be a part of a great team, you also need great individual performance. The culture change you are looking for is most easily adopted if there is a demonstrable area of success you can point to "Look how well it is working over here/there". Focus on doing your job fantastically as a department, THEN take it out to share it with the entire company.

Even with this process it is difficult to push outside your area of control and exact change elsewhere, you need allies in high places. But cultural change, like any change or movement, needs to start somewhere, and if no one starts, it will never happen.

The Verdict:

Silo until you have your stuff together, then start bringing people in and reaching out. Oftentimes the enormity of the "company" can overwhelm your staff, leaving them with a feeling of helplessness "Even if we get our stuff right, there's so much out there that is messed up". Once you have a strong basis of excellence as support to point to, then open up. But let it happen naturally and slowly, if you go around touting your success, you inspire defensiveness in others. Word of any success in a company will spread, and that gives you practice in shoring up and protecting what you have built as people come to you with questions and challenges. From these interactions you can begin to build a roadmap for others, and thus become a leader within your organization.

A Cluttered Desk, Good or Bad?

"A cluttered desk is the sign of a cluttered mind" ~*Anonymous*

"If a cluttered desk is a sign of a cluttered mind, of what, then, is an empty desk a sign?" ~*Albert Einstein*

.　　.　　.　　.　　.

So which is it? To clutter or not to clutter? There are those who believe that a cluttered desk is the sign of someone who is working hard, and while I understand that perception, what makes a greater impression is being good at what you do. If you are relying on your desk to make the impression that you are working hard, you probably have bigger problems.

Another constructive argument is that you should have bigger priorities than cleaning your desk. This is absolutely the case, but the argument against is that it takes little time to keep an organized workspace if done even once a month.

And in regards to Einstein above, I believe he was simply making a statement in regards to a desk being a poor way of measuring someone's intellect, not necessarily weighing in on the question we have before us (he was smarter than to jump in the middle of this hot topic). So what are the main points of the cluttered side and neat side of the argument?

The Tidy Desk Argument

- *Eliminates distraction* – Personally, there is nothing more distracting for me than the HUGE amount of work that is constantly ahead of me to do. In your building, the most important space for you is your desk. By keeping the reminders, post-it notes, and stacks of paperwork away from my immediate view, you are able to focus more on what needs to be done right now.
- *Forces you to delegate or discard* – My second favorite thing about a clean workspace is forcing me to get some of the work off of my plate. If you know you have higher priorities when you pick up that next file, it's a great time to pass that along to someone else. Just as likely, you may find that the work has already been done, or no longer needs doing (the lowest priority items are often like that).
- *Sets an orderly tone for your department* – For me this is the most important benefit of all. If everyone sees that I have my work in order, it is easier for me to expect that everyone else have their work in order as well. It helps set the expectation of organization.
- *Judgment* – Whether it be your boss or your coworkers, people naturally judge, and in the open environment of most workplaces today, if your desk is piled with stacks of paper and general disorder, rightly or wrongly, that can be taken as a sign of being lazy, ineffective, and undisciplined

The "Organization" Myth of your desk

Notice that I didn't put, "Being able to find things" in the space above. In my experience, even a messy desk has some thought process behind it and the person is almost always able to find the information they are looking for in short order. It is just as likely that the person who keeps an orderly desk cannot remember exactly where they filed away that document from last week as it is that the person who keeps a messy desk can't remember which pile of paper it is in.

The Cluttered Desk Argument

- *Cleaning is a "low value" activity* – Unless you absolutely need to equate cleanliness with organization , your time can be more valuably spent elsewhere. This is the central argument of anyone whose desk is cluttered. "I've got better things to do with my time, and I bet you do as well".
- *Procrastination* – Similar to the above argument, for many people, tidying up the desk is just a way to look productive while they are in reality just procrastinating from doing the work they really should be doing.
- *Keeping a "clean desk" is itself a distraction* – If you're always worried about keeping everything in order, then you are taking your eye off of the ball and losing focus on your work.
- *Helps keep track of workload* –By not "hiding" anything away where I can't see it, I am always able to see what I have to work on, can prioritize on the fly, and can't let anything slip "out of sight, out of mind"

The Verdict:

The fact is there is little to no downside in keeping a tidy workspace, which is why I almost always come down on the "neat desk" side of the argument. With that said, the answer is not yours alone to decide. Perceptions are very real in the workplace, and for better or for worse, can have an impact on your career advancement. Your boss is the ultimate arbiter of the question. Look to your boss's desk, the VP's desk, and even the CEO's desk for your answer. If you see a pattern of either tidiness or disarray, you probably have your answer regarding their expectation and what the correct answer of this issue is for you.

Tricks of the Trade

Who has time for cleaning? - For those who are concerned with the time it takes to clean, I find that I multi-task my way through most of the cleaning while on conference calls or other phone calls. Also, just setting up a once a week cleaning on Friday, for instance, can help keep most of the clutter build-up under control.

Manage the disarray – For those who are naturally a little more messy and work in an very neat and tidy office, or anyone looking to be a little more tidy for whatever reason, I recommend the following . Keep only a couple of piles of paperwork at most, organize one pile into several by "stacking" one pile vertically and the next horizontally, and/or keep the piles behind you, or even better, in an accessible drawer, file cabinet, or other out of sight piece of office furniture.

Either way, don't make it a "disorder" - My only caution is to not let it get out of hand one way or the other. As soon as you need to start piling stuff on the floor, you've probably gone too far on the disorder side. If you can't focus or work if you have anything on your desk, you're probably getting over the deep end of cleanliness. Find a balance that works for you, and the expectations of your company.

Should Your Goal Be Perfection?

"A good plan violently executed now is better than a perfect plan executed next week." ~George Patton

"Perfection is not attainable, but if we chase perfection we can catch excellence." ~Vince Lombardi

. . . . .

We talk a lot about striving for perfection, but sometimes perfection takes a whole lot more time and money than we think. So given that time and money are not unlimited resources the question is: When is less than perfect good enough? Or should "perfect" really be the only goal worth putting your efforts toward?

The Case for Good Enough, not Perfect

#1 - Perfection Delays the Benefit:

While it is imperative that you hold people accountable for delivering ALL of what you want them too, I've seen too many times where the benefit of a new system or process is delayed by months while the Project Manager or Department Manager strives for perfection. The most important question to ask is this:

What part of this can we use NOW while we keep perfecting the process/product?

Make immediate improvements whenever possible and refine/improve from there. This can have a lot of benefits; it lets the staff "ease into the waters", builds momentum for the project/process, and realizes a return on investment as soon as possible. But to dial it back to a more basic level, you need to ask a very basic question first:

Is the benefit of the system and process in its currently developed state an improvement?

- No – Well then it is easy, it still needs work. The question then becomes whether the money and time is worth continuing, or would be better spent somewhere else?
- Yes – Then the cost/benefit needs to be weighed against the improvements that could be realized by implementing right now. Can you implement now while you still work on it?

Don't get caught waiting for perfection when you are trying to implement a new process/project....you might be waiting a long time, and be missing out on a lot of benefits.

#2 - Striving for Perfection is Demoralizing:

Nothing can be more demoralizing for your staff than to work their tails off, succeed on all levels, crush the competition, yet still be told that they fell short because it wasn't perfect. You should strive for continued excellence, not for perfection. Perfection in this model is unattainable

The Case for Perfection

#1 - The only way to know what your "true north" goal is:

What are you really striving for? What are your benchmarks? This came to my mind while listening to a government awareness campaign on highway safety. The campaign was called "Zero Fatalities" and succinctly said that even one death a year wasn't OK, that nobody should die. Similar campaigns have rolled out at hospitals to track rates of infection.

In the business world, isn't one dissatisfied customer one too many? Shouldn't you do what you can to recover that customer? Shouldn't you learn something so that it doesn't happen again? Keeping the goal at "perfect" means that you won't say "Well 99 out of a hundred customers are satisfied, that's good enough", it clarifies what you are striving for.

#2 - Striving for perfection isn't demoralizing, it is inspiring:

People get a whole lot more excited about trying to hit a Home-Run vs. trying to hit a Single. Big lofty goals bring out the best in all of us. They focus our minds and require the greatest amount of effort. Just because you don't reach perfection, doesn't mean that you can't celebrate excellence, you just need to acknowledge that you still have work to do.

The Verdict:

Truthfully, I had personally always fallen along the lines of those who believed striving for perfection was a silly, arrogant, and demoralizing goal to go for. However, I have come around to a compromise.

Communicating the mission and purpose behind your actions is one of the first and most important attributes of a successful manager. Laying out the goal of "perfection" clarifies what actions your staff should take. The caveat to that is that you MUST set milestones along the way and celebrate the steps toward that goal. Perfection is the goal in airline maintenance and hospitals for example, why not your operation as well? Just don't be that boss that is never pleased, nobody likes that person.

Persistence vs. Stupidity

"Insanity: doing the same thing over and over again and expecting different results." ~Albert Einstein

"Try, try, try, and keep on trying is the rule that must be followed to become an expert in anything." ~W.Clement Stone

. . . . .

Just because you have spent a ton of time, money and effort on a project, does not mean you shouldn't re-evaluate it along the way. Leave your ego in the parking lot when you walk into work. Too often, we get attached to our projects and can't admit that our work has not been, or is not, as successful as we would like. In the worst case, it is an out and out failure.

Now I have a belief that things take three times longer to work than we think they will when we start the endeavor. But at what point do we stop? At what point does our persistence begin resembling stubbornness and stupidity? What we must find is the reasoning for why we are carrying on with our plan.

So what are some of the differentiators of persistence versus stupidity?

- *Never giving up* – There is a difference between never giving up on your goal, and never giving up on HOW you reach that goal. Persistence is maintaining flexibility on how you get to where you want to be. Stupidity is never acknowledging failure as a teacher.
- *Never re-evaluating success* – The other "persistence trap" is when faced with success. Lots of people accomplish what they want, but don't get the results they were after. Stupidity is just waiting for the results to change. Persistence is evaluating and learning from success with the same "enthusiasm" as learning from failure.
- *The effect of logic and people* – Persistence focuses solely on the results and the data that show whether their actions get the results they want. Stupidity is expecting everyone to do what is logical (please read into this; what WE think would be logical) and sticking with that course of action while waiting for everyone to "get it".

OK, so everyone knows the basics now, but what about the greyer areas and trying to identify as fast as you can whether you are starting to cross the persistent/stupid line. To that end, I recommend you answer two questions:

Question #1 - Is it working? Just slower than you had hoped:

- *How slowly* – Does the new anticipated end of the project make sense? The big question for new initiatives in the marketplace is whether the rate of change is growing at a compound rate, or a linear rate (are you adding 20 customers each day, or are you growing at 20, 21, 22, 23, 24, etc each day). If it is at the compound rate (the ever increasing one) then you can rest assured that you are on the right track, it may just take a while. If you are growing only at a steady rate, then you need to determine whether that rate is large enough to make further investment worthwhile.

- *Can your time be better spent elsewhere (Plan B)* – This is ALWAYS on the plate. If there is a more profitable way to spend your time, then you have an obligation to take it (realizing that to be profitable, you must FINISH something). So when a plan doesn't reach your expected level of success, maybe you can lock in what success you have had, then move on to something with higher upside for the time you need to spend.

Question #2 - Is it not working? Something must change:

- *Is it the product?* – What are the greatest issues of dissatisfaction? Is there a way to deal with all of them in a creative/new way or is it a laundry list of things to be tackled one at a time?
- *Is it a policy/procedure?* – Can it be done simpler? Is it changeable, or is it a regulation that can't be? Use what flexibility you have.
- *Is it employee/customer engagement?* – Are you reaching the right people? Are you communicating the important information?

The Verdict:

Don't get too attached to what you have spent your time on, there is a good chance you could do more for the company and yourself if you re-evaluate where you spend your effort. The real question is, have you learned from failure? Based on what you know NOW, can you build a roadmap to success? If you can't, or more likely, if your time could be better spent on another project, then lock in the gains you have, and move on. Don't get caught in the trap of beating your head against a wall.

The Manager's Diary

APPENDIX III

Top 100 Leadership & Management Quotes

Top 100 Leadership & Management Quotes

1. "A good leader is a person who takes a little more than his share of the blame and a little less than his share of the credit." ~John C Maxwell
2. "In the business world, everyone is paid in two coins: cash and experience. Take the experience first; the cash will come later." ~Harold Geneen
3. "Tell me and I forget. Teach me and I remember. Involve me and I learn." ~Benjamin Franklin
4. "It's better to hang out with people better than you. Pick people whose behavior is better than yours and you'll drift in that direction." ~Warren Buffett
5. "A pessimist is somebody who complains about the noise when opportunity knocks." ~Oscar Wilde
6. "Before you are a leader, success is all about growing yourself. When you become a leader, success is all about growing others." ~Jack Welch
7. "A man must be big enough to admit his mistakes, smart enough to profit from them, and strong enough to correct them." ~John C. Maxwell
8. "Never be afraid to try, remember, amateurs built the ark. Professionals built the Titanic." ~Dave Barry
9. "The key is not to prioritize what's on your schedule, but to schedule your priorities." ~ Stephen Covey
10. "A good manager is a man who isn't worried about his own career but rather the careers of those who work for him." ~H.S.M. Burns

11. "A leader is not an administrator who loves to run others, but one who carries water for his people so that they can get on with their jobs" ~Robert Townsend

12. "If you can't explain it simply, you don't understand it well enough." ~Albert Einstein

13. "If you want to go fast, go alone. If you want to go far, you need a team." ~John Wooden

14. "Leaders become great, not because of their power, but because of their ability to empower others." -John Maxwell

15. "If your actions inspire others to dream more, learn more, do more and become more, you are a leader." ~John Quincy Adams

16. "You don't get paid for the hour. You get paid for the value you bring to the hour." ~ J.Rohn

17. "Instead of worrying about what people say of you, why not spend time trying to accomplish something they will admire." ~ Dale Carnegie

18. "Leaders don't create followers, they create more leaders." ~Tom Peters

19. "I don't know the key to success, but the key to failure is trying to please everybody." ~ Bill Cosby

20. "Good leaders inspire people to have confidence in the leader. Great leaders inspire people to have confidence in themselves." ~Eleanor Roosevelt

21. "Continuous improvement is better than delayed perfection." ~Mark Twain

22. "The most important thing in communication is hearing what isn't said." ~Peter Drucker

23. "The pessimist complains about the wind. The optimist expects it to change. The Leader adjusts the sails." ~John C. Maxwell

24. "Vision without action is merely a dream. Action without vision just passes the time. Vision with action can change the world." ~Joel Barker

25. "You have to put in many, many, many tiny efforts that nobody sees or appreciates before you achieve anything worthwhile." ~Brian Tracy
26. Remember the difference between a boss and a leader; a boss says "Go!" - a leader says "Let's go!" ~E.M. Kelly
27. "People often say that motivation doesn't last. Well, neither does bathing - that's why we recommend it daily." ~Zig Ziglar
28. "Don't confuse motion and progress. A rocking horse keeps moving but doesn't make any progress." ~Alfred Montapert
29. "If you listen to your fears, you will die never knowing what a great person you might have been." ~Robert H. Schuller
30. "Empty pockets never held anyone back. Only empty heads and empty hearts can do that." ~Norman Vincent Peale
31. "Failure + failure + failure = success. You only fail when you quit." ~Jack Hyles
32. "Lead and inspire people. Don't try to manage and manipulate people. Inventories can be managed but people must be lead." — Ross Perot
33. "Discipline is doing what you really do not want to do, so you can do what you really want to do." ~John C. Maxwell
34. "Be clear about your goal but be flexible about the process of achieving it." ~ Brian Tracy
35. "One person with passion is better than forty people merely interested." ~E. M. Forster
36. "A successful man is one who can lay a firm foundation with the bricks others have thrown at him." ~David Brinkley
37. "It is not the employer who pays the wages. Employers only handle the money. It is the customer who pays the wages." ~Henry Ford

38. "There are no secrets to success. It is the result of preparation, hard work and learning from failure." ~Colin L. Powell

39. "Vision without execution is a daydream. Execution without vision is a nightmare." ~Japanese Proverb

40. "Good leaders create a vision, articulate the vision, passionately own the vision, and relentlessly drive it to completion." ~Jack Welch

41. "Hire character. Train skill." ~Peter Schutz

42. "You can tell whether a man is clever by his answers. You can tell whether a man is wise by his questions." ~Naguib Mahfouz

43. "The man who does things makes many mistakes, but he never makes the biggest mistake of all; doing nothing." ~Ben Franklin

44. "Success is a lousy teacher. It seduces smart people into thinking they can't lose." ~Bill Gates

45. "It's hard to beat a person who never gives up." ~Babe Ruth

46. "Nearly all men can stand adversity, but if you want to test a man's character, give him power." ~Abraham Lincoln

47. "If you don't have time to do it right, what makes you think you will have time to do it over?" ~Seth Godin

48. "If everyone has to think outside the box, maybe it is the box that needs fixing." ~Malcolm Gladwell

49. "It is not the strongest of the species that survive, nor the most intelligent, but the one most responsive to change." ~Charles Darwin

50. "Leadership is not just what happens when you're there, it's what happens when you're not there." ~Ken Blanchard

51. "Management is a position that is granted; leadership is a status that is earned." ~K. Scott Derrick

52. "Trying to get everyone to like you is a sign of mediocrity." ~Colin Powell

53. "I am more afraid of an army of one hundred sheep led by a lion than an army of one hundred lions led by a sheep." ~Charles Maurice

54. "I never look at the glass as half empty or half full. I look to see who is pouring the water and deal with them." ~Mark Cuban

55. "To succeed in life we must stay within our strength zone but move out of our comfort zone." ~John C. Maxwell

56. "Rules of Work: Out of clutter find simplicity; From discord find harmony; In the middle of difficulty lies opportunity." ~Albert Einstein

57. "If Columbus had turned back, no one would have blamed him. Of course, no one would have remembered him either." ~Unknown

58. "The harder I worked, the luckier I got." ~Thomas Jefferson

59. "Talent hits a target no one else can hit; Genius hits a target no one else can see." ~Arthur Schopenhauer

60. "If you have no critics you'll likely have no success." ~Malcolm Forbes

61. "The twin killers of success are impatience & greed." ~Jim Rohn

62. "One important key to success is self-confidence. An important key to self-confidence is preparation." ~Arthur Ashe

63. "Do the hard jobs first. The easy jobs will take care of themselves." ~Dale Carnegie

64. "Your job gives you authority. Your behavior gives you respect." ~ Irwin Federman

65. "Management is doing things right; leadership is doing the right things." ~Peter Drucker

66. "Some people dream of success while others wake up and work hard at it." ~Colin Powell

67. "The ability to learn faster than your competitors may be the only sustainable competitive advantage." ~Arie du Geus

68. "Experience is not what happens to a man; it is what a man does with what happens to him." ~Aldous Huxley

69. "Optimism is the faith that leads to achievement. Nothing can be done without hope & confidence." ~Helen Keller

70. "Patience, persistence and perspiration make an unbeatable combination for success." ~Napoleon Hill

71. "Two elements of successful leadership: a willingness to be wrong and an eagerness to admit it." ~Seth Godin

72. "Be careful the environment you choose for it will shape you; be careful the friends you choose for you will become like them." ~W. Clement Stone

73. "Great leaders are almost always great simplifiers who cut through argument, debate, and doubt to offer a solution everybody can understand." ~Colin Powell

74. "When people talk, listen completely. Most people never listen." ~Ernest Hemingway

75. "A culture of discipline is not a principle of business; it is a principle of greatness." ~Jim Collins

76. "Not everything that counts can be counted, and not everything that can be counted counts." ~Albert Einstein

77. "Don't judge each day by the harvest you reap but by the seeds that you plant." ~Robert Louis Stevenson

78. "Excellence is not an accomplishment. It is a spirit, a never-ending process." ~Lawrence M. Miller

79. "Quality means doing it right when no one is looking." ~Henry Ford

80. "I don't pay good wages because I have a lot of money; I have a lot of money because I pay good wages." ~Robert Bosch

81. "A clever person solves a problem. A wise person avoids it" ~Albert Einstein

82. "Successful people make the right decisions early and manage those decisions daily." ~John C. Maxwell
83. "Productivity is never an accident. It is always the result of a commitment to excellence, intelligent planning, and focused effort." ~Paul Meyer
84. "I cannot trust a man to control others who cannot control himself." ~ Robert E. Lee
85. "The first responsibility of a leader is to define reality. The last is to say thank you. In between, the leader is a servant." — ~Max DePree
86. "In the past a leader was a boss. Today leaders must be partners with their people. They no longer can lead based on positional power." ~Ken Blanchard
87. "Productivity is never an accident. It is always the result of a commitment to excellence, intelligent planning, and focused effort." ~Paul Meyer
88. "Experience is a hard teacher because she gives the test first, the lesson afterwards." ~Vernon Sanders Law
89. "I can accept failure, but I can't accept not trying." ~Michael Jordan
90. "The older I get the less I listen to what people say and the more I look at what they do." ~Andrew Carnegie
91. "Your most unhappy customers are your greatest source of learning." ~Bill Gates
92. "Your success will be the degree to which you build up others who work with you. While building up others, you build up yourself." ~James Casey
93. "Good leaders make people feel that they're at the very heart of things, not at the periphery." ~Warren Bennis
94. "As a leader, you're probably not doing a good job unless your employees can do a good impression of you when you're not around." ~Patrick Lencioni
95. "Do one thing every day that scares you." ~Eleanor Roosevelt
96. "I learned the best way to save face is to keep the bottom half of it shut." ~Unknown

97. "When it is obvious that the goals cannot be reached, don't adjust the goals, adjust the action steps." ~Confucius

98. "Simplicity is the ultimate sophistication" ~Leonardo da Vinci

99. "You get the best efforts from others not by lighting a fire beneath them, but by building a fire within." ~Bob Nelson

100. "Successful leaders see the opportunities in every difficulty rather than the difficulty in every opportunity." ~Reed Markham

Epilogue

One thing that I have noticed is that sometimes the lesson has been right in front of my face for me to learn, but I wasn't in the stage of my career where I could recognize it. For that reason I recommend you come back to this book periodically over your career and read it again. Some of the lessons contained within will jump out at you in ways they never did during this initial reading, and others will come at you from a different perspective. We are all at different points in our career and have been exposed to different experiences. I hope you'll revisit this book occasionally and see if it can continue to be a help to you.

22232579R00135

Made in the USA
Lexington, KY
18 April 2013